· ibs ·

Irritable Bowel Syndrome

·ibs·

Irritable Bowel Syndrome

A COMPREHENSIVE GUIDE
TO MANAGING AND IMPROVING
YOUR CONDITION
AND YOUR LIFE

Rachel Cooper

JSD INTERNATIONAL, INC.
NEW YORK

Illustrations by Evan Benvenisti
Photographs by Ed Haas
Model: Sandy Dell
Cover design by Cathy Morgan

10 9 8 7 6 5 4 3 2 1

Printed in the United States of America

with all my love and humble gratitude to
my family, and especially, my little
Jonathan

▪ contents ▪

▪ foreword ▪

Irritable bowel Syndrome (IBS) is a chronic condition of the gastrointestinal tract that affects a significant number of people in the United States. For a sufferer, IBS can manifest itself in any number of ways and it can develop across the lifespan, including during childhood. Some may suffer with diarrhea while others may experience constipation for extended time periods.

The common thread for those living with IBS is that their gastrointestinal tract becomes over-stimulated and over-reactive to diet or stress or a combination of the two. The unfortunate predicament of IBS is pain, discomfort and associated embarrassment. The good news with IBS is, while there is no cure, IBS can be treated and does not necessarily lead to other more serious medical conditions.

This book will provide valuable information that will enable you to take a proactive approach to improving your condition as well as better your general health and wellness. Coupled with ongoing medical care, this book offers a variety of suggestions to treat your whole self, the body as well as the mind. This is the critical part in understanding IBS, as it requires a patient educated along a wide spectrum concerning his or her personal health care issues. Medicating yourself when you have abdominal pain may provide symptom relief but does not address the underlying causative factors. For example, your stomachache may have begun prior to an anxiety-inducing event. If you delve further, you may find that this particular event occurs twice weekly with associated diarrhea. For others, it may be that Sunday family dinner that brings on a bout of constipation that drags on for days. These are the discovered "red flags" or "triggers" that come to awareness as you take charge of your illness. These are the issues or problems that ultimately need to be changed. This exercise in self-exploration is just the beginning of life alterations that may initially disrupt routine but ultimately lead to the reward of feeling better and functioning in a more productive fashion.

Learning about your condition is a large step toward managing your life with IBS. Use this book as a tool to gain many stress reduction approaches and life management skills. Be diligent in exploring the treatment modalities that have helped others with IBS and discover those techniques that are most advantageous. Have an awareness that diet, exercise and professional counseling alone or in tandem can make real and far-reaching differences in quality of life.

Trust that with education, hard work, and appropriate medical consultation you will learn to make the necessary changes in your lifestyle to help guarantee that you are on the road to wellness.

Hopefully, this book will provide you with initial guidance and ongoing strategies toward symptom relief and will educate you in maintaining a healthy and more content view toward living with IBS and life in general.

Peter Brancato, Jr., M.D.
Medical Director
Psychiatry, South Jersey Hospital System

∙ ibs ∙

Irritable Bowel Syndrome

• introduction •

Do you suffer from unexplainably frequent, perhaps chronic stomach pains? Do your pains consist of cramping, bloating, gas, and bouts of diarrhea and/or constipation? Does your daily life feel imposed upon by your symptoms? Perhaps you're always worried about finding a nearby bathroom while shopping, traveling, or even dining out. Do you think you're imagining it or, are you fearful that your discomfort is due to a serious disease? Has life become one horrible embarrassment? If so, **you are not alone.** In fact, several studies suggest that at least 25 percent of the American population suffers from what has come to be known as Irritable Bowel Syndrome (IBS), and this is just a *national* estimate. Globally, this figure may be four times that amount! Can you imagine how many people around the world are suffering just like you?

This book is meant to help you gain control over your medical situation, and ultimately, help you to gain greater control over your life. It is a tool that should not only help you to feel less awkward about your condition, but encourage you to find solutions. There is no question that IBS can make you feel badly about yourself. *First and foremost however, you should cease feeling ashamed about your condition.* Irritable Bowel Syndrome is as real as it is uncomfortable and both physically and emotionally exhausting.

Irritable Bowel Syndrome is a chronic condition of the gastrointestinal tract that affects approximately 35–55 million

Americans each year. The reason for such a broad figure is because statistics vary widely among general practitioners, doctors of internal medicine, and other health care practitioners. Until recently, people with IBS have suffered in silence. Here are some reasons why:

- **Embarrassment**: Most sufferers of IBS feel anxious about sharing their condition with others, including their physicians. It is understandable that discussing one's battle with gas, bloating, constipation, and/or diarrhea is difficult, particularly with peers. And imagine discussing these symptoms as a reason for avoiding plans with family and friends!
- **Self-Doubt**: Often those with IBS have a hard time taking their own problem seriously. Certainly they would rather not live with the pain, but frequently, what appears to be a repeated visit to the doctor because of a "stomach ache," seems "silly," or redundant, pointless, and costly. "Perhaps if I ignore it," people often rationalize, "it will go away." All too often, people try to ignore their symptoms because they think that they are imagining them. If you're hurting, do you think that you could *really* be *imagining* it?
- **Lack of Validation**: For quite some time, some doctors suggested that IBS was strictly a psychological problem rather than a physical one, or a combination of the two. If IBS sufferers *did* make it to the doctor, they often found that they were turned away with perhaps a pat on the back and the affirmation that something more serious was *not* going on. Although this was reassuring, it did not soothe the patient for long and the discomfort of the symptoms remained. Eventually, many sufferers believed there was no help to be found anywhere and certainly very few sympathetic people to lean on.

However, in the last ten years or so, studies have indicated that up to half of all visits to the offices of gastroenterologists have been due to what is now commonly known as Irritable Bowel Syndrome. Although such a vast number of IBS sufferers have sought medical help and evaluation, they are left with the conclusion that there is nothing wrong. Patients are often sent home with empty reassurance. This, of course, is good news. The bad news is that the symptoms persist. The unfortunate truth is that IBS is not a curable condition. It is also not a condition that one need suffer terribly from on a regular basis. If you are a sufferer, there is a lot that can be done to improve the quality of your life, and help to alleviate some of your uncomfortable, often painful, and embarrassing symptoms.

This book will explore the reasons you may be suffering from IBS and help you to understand ways in which you can improve your condition and the quality of your life. The steps that you yourself can take to control your symptoms will help significantly to reduce the impact IBS has on your physical wellness and social existence. You *can* make changes that may profoundly affect the way you feel. Although IBS may be a part of your life, there are many ways to live with it and still feel great. **The goal of this book is to help *you* help *yourself*.**

It is most important, however, that you understand this book is not a substitute for medical advice. You are urged to consult with a physician before practicing any dietary or exercise program. Only your doctor can provide you with a sound diagnosis and an appropriate recommendation on ways to proceed in treating IBS or any other condition.

For many of you, reading this book may be the first step you have taken to seriously address your condition. Although the information presented is a compilation of studies and opinions of physicians and specialists, it is important to know that the very nature of IBS offers a variety of conclusions and differing opinions. Many doctors can come up with different explanations. It is important that you seek medical help that will validate your feelings. In addition, your doctor should spend as much time as necessary to aid in your search for solutions. Keep this in mind as you read. Not all treatments suggested here in this text are right for you but through a little self-evaluation, you can create a "formula" of daily modifications that can dramatically improve your condition and your life! Be patient! Learning to live well with IBS requires that you learn to experiment with the tools you will become familiar with here in this text. While some tactics will work, others won't. Often, variations of tactics are the most effective. Ultimately, in time, you will have explored enough to know what is right for you. Hang in there, whatever you do! Change takes time, but the benefits are well worth the wait!

· one ·

Why Does *My Stomach Always Hurt?*
What Is Irritable Bowel Syndrome?

It is not so easy to come up with a concise definition of Irritable Bowel Syndrome. IBS is one of those ailments that have a range of defining properties which have changed and expanded over the years. Curious, isn't it? Who would have thought such a common ailment could be so hard to define!

Simply put, IBS is an extremely common disorder of the intestines, not the stomach, although this is a common misperception. For a sufferer, IBS manifests itself in the gastrointestinal tract (GI tract)—which is partially composed of the colon, also known as the large intestine, and small intestine— in any combination of ways. These manifestations may include gassiness, cramping, and bloating, as well as diarrhea and/or constipation. Some IBS patients suffer more often with diarrhea. Others find that constipation is how IBS presents itself. In addition, IBS symptoms should occur for at least ten days and reoccur with seemingly haphazard regularity. For example, you may exhibit these symptoms for up to two weeks in a row, and then again for another week with a five-day reprieve in between. Strangely, there is neither rhyme nor reason to when or how severely IBS will emerge. In addition, there is no telling how long a bout will last. This is one of the most bothersome aspects of IBS for those who live with it. As of now, the cause of IBS is unknown and there is no cure.

Historically, IBS has been called a variety of things, including spastic bowel, functional bowel disease, spastic colon, colitis, and mucous colitis. Many of these names are in fact inaccurate. For example, colitis, or ulcerative colitis, actually means inflammation or swelling of the colon, and is often marked by blood in the stool; IBS causes no such condition. Similarly, Crohn's Disease, another nonspecific inflammatory condition affecting the intestines or colon is, medically speaking, more serious than IBS. Generally, doctors refer to IBS as a "functional disorder" because in fact, the colon shows no sign of disease at all upon examination.

In addition to discomfort as a result of gas and bloating, the condition itself often causes intense pain in the abdomen, and that is unfortunately, not all. Periods of irregular, atypical bowel movements also occur. For some sufferers, IBS may include infrequent or difficult bowel movements, otherwise known as constipation. For these sufferers this type of discomfort is dreadful. Plagued with bloating and the feeling of needing "to go," these patients can suffer from headaches and backaches as well, which believe it or not, are also a result of constipation.

For others, the pain and inconvenience of diarrhea or frequent loose stools is the way IBS exhibits itself. This type of IBS is just as bad. Pain, gas, and chronic diarrhea can also lead to lethargy and dehydration. It is important to note here that, for some people, it is normal to not produce a bowel movement every day. Do not be alarmed if you only excrete feces every three or four days, for example. This may be normal for you! If you have moved your bowels every other day (for example) for as long as you can remember and you no longer do so, nor have you for an extended period of time, then you have cause to be concerned. If, perhaps, every other day you produced a normal bowel movement and now it seems as though you are constipated for several days before you produce a painful bowel movement, this is reason to wonder. If you have moved your bowels normally on a daily basis for years, but now seem to battle diarrhea for at least five days this, too, is cause for concern and reason enough to visit your physician.

Strangely, although those with IBS contend with such specific physical discomfort, tests generally show no disease, swelling, or infection of the colon or intestines. Rather, it may be that the nerves of these sufferers are particularly sensitive to certain foods; even emotional conflict or stress can induce painful spasms in the muscles of the intestines, eventually leading to irregular bowel movements and other symptoms. Perhaps you've noticed that after eating certain foods you are stricken with terrible diarrhea or painful bloating. It may be common for you to experience chronic, unexplainable intestinal cramps and/or constipation when forced to deal with a stressful situation.

The problem with identifying IBS is that no one, not even your doctor, may know for sure what is at the root of your colon hypersensitivity. Diet and stress have been shown to be major influencing factors, however, and will be further explored later in the book. And, although this text will help you find ways to manipulate your digestive system to your advantage, it is most important that you visit your doctor so that he or she may conduct tests that will exclude the possibility of more serious diseases. It is important to remember that suffering from IBS **does not** mean that you have or will develop a more serious chronic condition. But only your doctor can assure you that IBS is—although uncomfortable—all you suffer from.

· two ·

How Should I Be Feeling?
Understanding How Digestion Works

So that your condition may make more sense to you, it is helpful to understand what is going on in your body as you digest food. Without IBS, digestion is not something one is even aware of! You should simply be able to eat a meal or snack, enjoy every last bite, and carry on with your day. You would not normally be aware of the secretion of acids, the breakdown of food within your stomach and intestines, and the eventual pushing and churning that the muscles of your colon use in order to push food out of your body. Eventually, when your intestines are left with nothing but waste, you would expel what you had consumed in the form of liquid (urine), or a bowel movement. It is important to note however, that expelling gas throughout the day, either orally or anally, is a perfectly normal function and unrelated to IBS. In fact, persons without IBS may expel up to 1–3 pints of gas a day. This is *normal* and *not* solely indicative of a more serious condition.

If you suffer from IBS, however, you may experience a range of discomfort soon after eating. Perhaps a specific type of food triggers your symptoms. Not long after eating, you may experience terrible bloating, painful gas, and a desire to move your bowels, which may prove to be unsuccessful. It is also possible that you find yourself unable to leave the nearest bathroom because of a bout of diarrhea.

Believe it or not, digestion begins as soon as you put food or liquid into your mouth. There are three major aspects of digestion that overlap during the course of proper digestive functioning: mixing, movement, and chemical breakdown.

❖ **Mixing** is essentially chewing your food just before you swallow, although in other parts of the digestive tract, mixing will occur again. Even before you place a piece of food into your mouth, your brain informs your salivary glands to begin excreting saliva so that it may assist in the process of breaking the food down into smaller bits and pieces. The enzyme released in your mouth by your salivary glands breaks down the compounds of starchy foods into smaller bits. Certainly, the smell of warm, freshly baked cookies has made your "mouth water." Well, that is what's supposed to happen. If, by looking at the cookies, your brain knows that you will take a bite out of one, it also knows that your mouth should be ready to receive that warm, soft, sweetness. Your mouth, after taking that bite and beginning to chew, is ready to alert your esophagus, stomach, and intestines that food is on the way.

▪ ▪ ▪

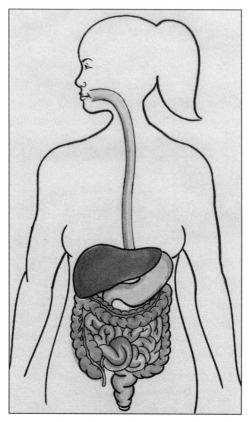

The digestive tract, including the small intestine
and colon (large intestine)

❖ The **movement** aspect of the digestion process is
strictly involuntary (i.e., you cannot control it). Unlike
chewing, once food is swallowed, the movement
process begins. Although the walls of the digestive system are hollow, they contain strong muscles that push
food and liquid into all necessary organs. Once food or
liquid passes through your throat, it enters the esophagus and is pushed by the muscles of the esophagus
down into the stomach. Imagine your fingers pushing

and squeezing water from one end of a sponge down to the other end. In essence, the muscular movement of the esophagus does just that. This movement, called peristalsis, permits food to pass through the esophagus until it reaches the entrance to the stomach where a muscular valvelike closure between the esophagus and stomach relaxes—thereby allowing food to comfortably pass down into the stomach. Here, in the stomach, some chemical breakdown occurs, similar to the type that occurs in the mouth. In the stomach, however, the digestive juices contain an acid that breaks down protein substances. To begin the process, the stomach has to contain the food and/or liquid it has received. This means that the upper portion of the stomach has to relax enough for substantial amounts of food to be accepted. Next, the food and liquid is mixed together with the digestive juices secreted by the stomach itself. Finally, through muscle movement, the mixed food portions and stomach juices are thoroughly combined in the lower portion of the stomach before it is pushed down into the small intestine, emptying the stomach.

❖ **Chemical breakdown** has now occurred both in the mouth, with the assistance of saliva, and again in the stomach, with the assistance of acidic stomach juices. Once the stomach has emptied its contents into the small intestine the juices of the pancreas and the liver (namely bile, which dilutes the fat content of the food), combine to break down fat, carbohydrates, and more proteins. Eventually, the digested nutrients are absorbed into the body through the intestinal walls while the remaining waste of the entire digestive process (including undigested food, otherwise known as fiber) are pushed into the bottom of the colon where it remains until it is expelled in the form of a bowel movement.

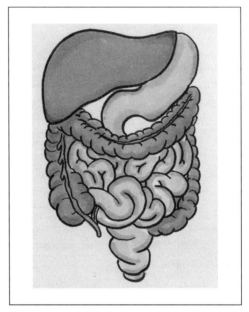

Close-up of the colon

The above list is a brief explanation of normal digestion. One of the most interesting aspects of the digestive system is its ability to regulate or control itself, which it does using both hormone and nerve regulators.

The hormone regulators are released by the lining of the stomach and small intestine. These regulators, or cells, begin their journey into the blood of the digestive tract, move to the heart and major arteries in the body and then return into the digestive tract where they encourage the production of digestive juices. Each digestive hormone—namely gastrin, secretin, and CCK (cholecystokinin)—serves a specific function within the digestive tract. While gastrin helps the stomach stimulate acid that dissolves and digests, secretin demands that the pancreas produce a bicarbonate-rich digestive juice that digests protein. Secretin also encourages the liver to produce the bile that is so important in aiding in successful digestion. CCK enables the pancreas to grow and develop. In addition, CCK helps the gallbladder to empty itself while also producing the enzymes that make up the pancreatic juice.

Equally important are the nerve regulators controlling the digestive system. The nerve regulators are quite interesting because they maintain the movement and pace of the digestive system. Two sets of nerves control this digestive action. They are called the extrinsic and intrinsic or the outside and inside nerves, respectively. The extrinsic nerves are based in the spinal cord and release two chemicals, adrenaline and acetylcholine. Although we tend to think of adrenaline as a chemical that works to stimulate our behavior, it actually works in an opposite fashion within our digestive system. Here, adrenaline relaxes the stomach muscles and muscles of the intestines and decreases the blood flow to these organs. Acetylcholine enables the muscles of the digestive organs to squeeze, thereby encouraging the forced flow, or push, of food through the digestive tract.

If you suffer from IBS, you cannot take digestion for granted. On the contrary, digestion may be uncomfortable, and often painful, embarrassing, and difficult to explain. For some reason, those with IBS have an especially sensitive colon and, as food passes through the intestines during the digestive process, this sensitivity triggers abdominal bloating, diarrhea, and/or constipation among other symptoms.

Keep in mind that regular bowel movements should be painless, bloodless, and without evidence of mucous. If painful bloating and cramping occur regularly before or during a bowel movement, this is probably indicative of a problem and you should share this information with your physician.

·three·

Do I Have IBS?
How Can I Know For Sure?

If you suspect that you suffer from IBS, you should visit your physician without delay so that a diagnosis may be confirmed and any other illness be ruled out. You should not be afraid to discuss your concerns. It may surprise you to know that a great number of people share your ailment. Most assuredly, you will *not* be the first patient your doctor has seen who complains of these symptoms.

Once you find yourself at your physician's office, you should be as open and honest as you can about your condition. You can only get the medical help you require, if you are upfront and uninhibited with your doctor. Don't be shy—your doctor has undoubtedly heard it all! You should expect your physician to ask a number of in-depth questions concerning your current ailment and medical history. Your doctor should inquire about the length of time your symptoms have persisted. Remember: IBS tends to last from five to ten days at a stretch and recur sporadically. Your doctor will want you to describe your constipation and/or diarrhea, the duration of these irregular bowel movements, your eating habits, and any over-the-counter or prescribed medication you may be taking, including herbal supplements and vitamins. In addition, you should share any information about your exercise habits, the level of your alcohol consumption, and nicotine usage, as well as any recreational drugs. It is also important that you let your doctor know about any family history of related medical problems, including colon cancer and colitis. Also remember to mention your fiber intake. Do you consume an enormous amount of fruit and vegetables or take a fiber supplement? It is necessary for your doctor to know this as well. Your fiber intake may be too high and may be triggering IBS symptoms that you need not suffer from!

It is also crucial to let your doctor know if you take laxatives on a regular basis. If you frequently take laxatives because you suffer from chronic constipation or because you are trying to control your weight (as many young people will resort to), please stop at once! Overuse of the stimulants found in laxatives could drastically alter the way your colon functions. Depending on laxatives to move your bowels will cause them to cease their ability to move successfully on their own. In addition, the force with which laxatives cause your bowels to move can alter your digestive process to such an extent that you may no longer be able to absorb necessary nutrients into the bloodstream before they are excreted out of your system. Your entire immune system can suffer as a result of laxative abuse! You should stop taking laxatives, unless already prescribed and monitored by a physician.

Feel free to share any information, whether it seems pertinent or not, about your family history of disease. Like a detective trying to solve a case, your doctor has to obtain as much information as she can about your body and its history so that she may rule out more serious conditions. Again, don't be afraid to be honest! It could make all the difference!

Once your history has been taken, you should expect a brief and mildly invasive examination. You may have blood taken as well as a rectal examination. As unpleasant as it sounds, rest assured, it is quick and painless. Your doctor will gently insert a gloved and lubricated finger into the rectum to test the tone of the muscles surrounding the anus and to obtain a fecal sample so that your stool may be tested for blood. It only takes a moment and will enable your doctor to get the most accurate results. Just try to relax. It's over before you know it. And, it may change your life!

If your symptoms sound more serious to your physician, he may ask that you submit to any number of diagnostic colorectal exams. These tests include: a colorectal transit test, a sigmoidoscopy or a colonoscopy, a barium enema X ray, and an anorectal function exam. Some diagnostic exams may also rule out diseases such as colon cancer.

❖ **Colorectal Transit Test**
   This test is particular to those IBS sufferers with chronic constipation. It is meant to find out how food moves through the colon. In this case, the patient must take a pill containing small markers, or spots, which can be viewed on X ray. In addition, the patient must follow a fairly high fiber diet for a period of time that encourages frequent muscle movement throughout the digestive process. The pace and movement of the markers is scanned and recorded several times over the course of approximately one week.

❖ **Sigmoidoscopy or Colonoscopy**
   A sigmoidoscopy involves the examination of the rectum and lower colon while a colonoscopy explores and examines the entire colon, or intestines. A sigmoidoscopy is generally performed when there is evidence of rectal bleeding, discharge, and pain. Medication is usually not necessary prior to the procedure; however, an enema may be given in order to cleanse and empty

the rectum. After rectal cleansing, a lubricated instrument with a light on the end of the inserted tip is gently pushed into the rectum for internal exploration. This often causes the patient to feel as though they need to make a bowel movement but, if performed by a specialist, should cause no pain.

Because a colonoscopy involves a deeper exploration of the colon, the patient is often given a mild sedative as well as an enema to cleanse the rectum. This is followed again by the insertion of a colonoscope through the rectum while the patient lies on his or her side. Air is then passed through the instrument in order to clearly explore the entire colon. This insertion of air may cause the patient to feel bloated and/or cramped. The discomfort will dissipate soon after the completion of the procedure. If an abnormality is discovered, a tissue sample will be taken for biopsy, or further evaluation. Again, it is a mildly uncomfortable process that will not take long.

❖ **Barium Enema X Ray**
The barium X ray is used to visually locate any obstruction or blockage within the colon. Before beginning this procedure, the patient needs to cleanse their colon thoroughly to avoid missing any crucial areas during the exam. The preparation, or bowel cleansing, requires drinking a full glass of a special liquid every fifteen minutes for roughly four hours the night before. Just prior to the process, your physician will fill your colon with an opaque liquid that makes your organs easier to see on X ray. This exam, like similar ones may result in some cramping and/or bloating that will dissipate soon after completion.

❖ **Anorectal Function Test**
The anorectal function test is meant to discover any abnormalities of the rectum, which may lead to chronic constipation. The exam mimics a bowel movement by

having your physician insert an air-filled balloon into the anus and then slowly retrieve it, or pull it back. It tests muscle tone and strength of contractual movement.

The aforementioned information, although seemingly filled with diagnostic language and even uncomfortably graphic imagery is not, by any means, meant to scare you! On the contrary, it is meant to make clear what to expect as you go through the diagnostic process. It is important to know that it is highly unlikely that you will have to undergo any tests unless you exhibit *severe* symptoms for an especially long period of time. If you suffer from IBS, it is quite possible your doctor will determine this without relying on an invasive examination. Most people with IBS do not need this extensive testing and find that they can be diagnosed after a medical history is obtained and physical examination given. It cannot be stressed enough, however, that if you think you may be suffering from IBS or any other serious condition, share this information with your physician openly and honestly.

·four·

Lactose Intolerance

Understanding the body's ability to digest carbohydrates is of utmost importance when the term "lactose intolerance" is suggested as a reason for your physical discomfort. Like IBS, lactose intolerance is a specific condition that also affects millions of people around the world and can exhibit many of the same symptoms. However it is *not* the same condition. This chapter is included in the book because you may in fact suffer from lactose intolerance instead of, or in addition to, IBS. If you suffer from an inability to digest certain carbohydrates, you need to make significant dietary changes, which will improve your health almost immediately.

If you are lactose intolerant, your body is unable to digest a sugar called lactose. Lactose is found predominately in milk, but is also contained in other dairy products. Interestingly, many of the symptoms exhibited in IBS patients are similar to

those of people who are lactose intolerant. These symptoms include: bloating, cramps, diarrhea, and sometimes nausea. When you are unable to digest lactose-rich foods and beverages it is because your body is lacking sufficient *lactase*, an enzyme prevalent in the small intestine. Lactase is necessary to break down the sugar lactose into a smaller form so that it may be absorbed by the body. Without the necessary amount of lactase, much of the lactose you ingest may end up undiluted in the large intestine. Food that is undiluted, or food which remains in larger pieces, can mix with various bacteria and form excess gas, creating the terrible bloat and discomfort you may experience. Without lactase, the body's attempt to break down lactose can be enormously discomforting. For most individuals being lactose intolerant is generally not dangerous.

The reasons for being lactose intolerant are as mysterious as the condition itself. Not so different from IBS, is it? On very rare occasions, infants are born lacking the ability to produce the lactase enzyme. This condition is generally discovered quickly and by and large will not affect those children who are nursing. For those babies not breast-fed, soy products are often substituted for milk products. These children, rest assured, are just as healthy as those fed cow's-milk-based formulas. As with all other infants, pediatricians should monitor these children closely and regularly in order to ensure that sufficient weight gain and healthy development is taking place.

Strange as it may seem, your ethnic background has a lot to do with your ability to produce lactase. Those most commonly afflicted with lactose intolerance are of Asian, African, or Native-American descent; up to 80 percent of these populations are lactose intolerant! If you are of Mediterranean descent (from Southern Italy or Greece), for example, you may also suffer from lactose intolerance although these numbers are not quite as high. Those of Northern European background are the least susceptible to this condition. Your ethnicity and race are not the only determining factors in developing lactose intolerance.

Perhaps you've noticed that you can no longer drink as much milk as you used to. Maybe that delicious cheese omelet you once loved has become torture to eat, and lately you find that you're spending much more time in the bathroom. Age may be the culprit. Believe it or not, the body produces less and less of the lactase needed to digest lactose as you get older. By the time you reach adolescence you may find milk and similar lactose-rich foods to be quite irritating to your GI tract. In adulthood you may be unable to drink milk at all. Luckily you can now find lactose-free milk and a variety of lactose-reduced products in your local supermarket.

Finally, and very importantly, specific diseases or medications can force the body to cease its production of lactase or, at the very least, significantly reduce it. If you think that any medication you may be taking has affected your ability to digest lactose with ease, speak to your doctor but *do not* stop taking your medication unless you are told to do so by your physician!

Understand that the more lactose you consume, the more severe your symptoms may be. With this in mind, it is advisable to reduce your lactose intake as soon as possible and see how you feel after doing so. You can experiment on your own to test your degree of discomfort. Pay attention to the amount of dairy you consume in a day. Writing down your consumption of dairy products will prove helpful. Keep a record of everything from the milk in your coffee to the cheese on your sandwich. Do you have cereal with milk for breakfast? A slice of cheese for a snack? Is ice cream your favorite dessert? How about butter or sour cream on your baked potato? You may be surprised at the amount of dairy you consume on an average day, and again, the more you consume, the greater your reaction may be to it.

The examples mentioned above are those lactose-rich foods that come to mind easily when you think of dairy items. However, there are many more foods containing small amounts of lactose that may still induce an uncomfortable response. Candies, instant soups and potatoes, salad dressings, cakes, cookies, bread, crackers, and luncheon meats may include enough lactose to create painful symptoms.

Keep in mind all foods that contain lactose as you experiment with lactose reduction in your diet. If you find that your symptoms do not begin to subside almost immediately, your condition may not be related to lactose intolerance at all and so you should speak with your physician as soon as possible. Your doctor may decide to administer one of several simple tests that will aid in finding the cause of your discomfort.

The **hydrogen breath test** measures the amount of hydrogen evident in your breath. Bacteria that are able to produce several gases, including hydrogen, may ferment lactose that remains in the colon undigested. After some time, this hydrogen is absorbed into the bloodstream. When it finally makes its way into the lungs, a problem may be detected when one exhales. While those who *can* digest lactose will not produce excess hydrogen upon exhalation, those who *are* intolerant will produce raised levels of hydrogen over a period of time. During the duration of the hydrogen breath test, the breath of the patient is tested at regular intervals after the patient has ingested a lactose-rich beverage. This test should *not* be given to very young children suspected of being lactose intolerant, as ingesting large amounts of lactose may be particularly harmful to them.

Another test for lactose intolerance requires the taking and testing of blood. Before giving blood for examination, you must fast for a specified time and then ingest a lactose-rich drink. Several samples of blood will be taken over a period of approximately two hours and the level of blood sugar will be measured. This reading indicates how successfully your body handles, or digests, lactose.

The final option for testing lactose intolerance requires a stool sample. This test is often reserved for infants and small children. If one tests positive for lactose intolerance, fermented, undigested lactose and/or glucose will be found in the stool.

Believe it or not, if it is discovered that you are in fact lactose intolerant, consider yourself fortunate. Learning to live with your condition is not as challenging as you might think. Although your body will not be able to change its inability to produce lactase, your awareness and decision-making will make a marked difference in the way your body responds to the foods you eat!

There are several ways to approach your intolerance to lactose and each solution depends in large part to your age and/or the severity of your responses to lactose. If you have an infant or toddler who is lactose intolerant you should avoid serving your child any foods or beverages that contain it. It is always best to err on the side of caution when dealing with an especially young child. For older children, young adults, and older adults, it is a good idea to monitor lactose intake, and responses to it, over several days before proceeding with a change in diet. Once you have an idea of your degree of responses to various lactose-rich foods, you can begin to reduce and/or substitute these items. You may find that certain foods bring on more severe reactions while others produce barely any. Milk and cheese may cause excess gas, bloating, and diarrhea while yogurt is digested with seemingly no response. Yogurt is one lactose-rich food that causes the least response in patients with lactose intolerance because of the active enzymes naturally existing in yogurt cultures that aid in digestion.

Soy-based foods and beverages are a great substitute for products made from cow's milk, such as butter and cheese. Not only are these soy-based foods healthful, they are also very tasty! More suggestions for these foods will be shared later. In addition to eliminating or substituting, you may also consider using lactase supplements to be taken just before or after a lactose-rich meal. These supplements are solely used to help you digest those lactose-rich foods that cause discomfort upon digestion. They can be particularly helpful when special occasions arise (like holidays) and being cautious about eating lactose-rich foods could prove difficult. These dietary aids can be found over the counter at your local grocery store or pharmacy.

Many of you reading this may be concerned with the potential lack of calcium in your diet if you take steps to change your eating habits in pursuit of better digestion. Don't worry! There are several ways to get the calcium required for your age group and improve your health.

Dark green, leafy vegetables (e.g., broccoli, collard greens, spinach, and kale), are a wonderful source of calcium, as are fish rich in oil, such as salmon. Most local drug stores offer daily calcium supplements if this solution is more practical for you.

Ultimately, the key to feeling better lies in monitoring your responses, seeing your physician, and proceeding with dietary alterations. If you are exclusively lactose intolerant, you can make yourself feel better when you commit to changing the way you eat. If your intolerance is coupled with IBS there are additional courses of action.

·five·

Stress and Your Stomach

IBS is a very real reaction to the challenges of everyday life. Stress is probably the single biggest contributor to IBS and it is important to understand how it affects different people in different ways. Although you may think your daily activities are not physically daunting, your health may be compromised in more ways than you imagined. It does not take a major life crisis, like the death of a loved one, to put your nerves on edge. Perhaps it's worrying about monthly expenses or even a commute to the office that gets your insides spinning. You may be going through a divorce which, amicable or not, is terribly traumatic. You may be unhappy at work, about to retire, or ready to begin college. Several examples of stress inducers are seemingly exciting and positive and you may wonder why something so hopeful and promising could be making you sick! Imagine a wedding. Such a significant and happy time in one's life can be dreadfully worrisome! When you really stop to think about it, there is so much in our lives, good and bad, that can cause us to feel an enormous amount of pressure and anxiety. Do not take for granted the fact that your problems may not appear to be as grave as someone else's. Although this may be true, it does not mean that the daily challenges of life are not taking a toll on your GI tract.

This is not meant to suggest that your condition is solely a response to life's pressures. In fact, quite the contrary is true. Understand that your body and mind work in tandem and outside influences can have a great impact on how your insides are feeling. It is no mistake that you more often notice how external factors impact your stomach and colon, rather than your Achilles tendons or your lymph glands. When you feel nervous, or worried, perhaps you have said, "I have butterflies in my stomach!" or "I feel sick to my stomach." Of course, there are no butterflies in your belly and you are probably not diagnostically ill at that moment. Rather, whatever you are responding to on the outside has caused you to feel it on the inside. Your stomach, or your colon are crying for help.

Up until recently, some doctors felt that IBS was strictly a psychosomatic condition, one where patients complained of symptoms that might not be real. Because physicians could not find a physical explanation they attributed the symptoms to the patient's imagination. Now, we know that while very little may be found to be physically impaired in the colon of an IBS patient, the symptoms do exist. It is very likely that the outside stresses in your life may manifest in many physical ways and can prove detrimental to your health.

When you're under stress or overly excited, the body often produces an unusually high level of adrenaline, which surges into the nerves of your colon. An adrenaline surge is what you feel when you're running a race, about to perform on stage, or surprised by a birthday celebration, among other examples. Adrenaline can make you feel a rush of energy and/or nervous excitement. When adrenaline works against you, the same energy you feel during a happy occasion can have the reverse effect when you're worried or stressed. This negative surge of adrenaline can, over time, make your GI tract very sensitive to things like physical or mental pressure, depression, and anxiety. If you recall in chapter 2, a good deal of movement, accompanied by relaxation, must occur for easy and successful digestion to take place. When outside conditions and poor dietary choices (to be discussed further in the following chapter) are inhibiting smooth digestion, it's no wonder that exposure to daily or more significant stresses may exacerbate or trigger your symptoms.

Sometimes the simplest medical treatments offer the best remedies. Perhaps you've heard the doctor's cliché about a patient who complains how much his foot hurts every time he jumps up and down. "Well, stop jumping up and down!" the doctor replies. It seems too simple, too easy, and yet it makes sense. Occasionally, you need to consider ways to reduce the pressures you face on a daily basis. Simple changes can have a significant impact on your mental and physical wellness. Stress may not be the *only* reason you are suffering from IBS, but it is an important one and it may be the easiest to understand.

Interestingly, IBS often begins around the age of adolescence. If you think about it, this is a time of great pressure, both external and self-induced. Young people, especially pre-adolescent girls, tend to put a tremendous amount of pressure on themselves to simultaneously assert their individuality and also fit-in with the "in crowd" all at once. It is a time of physical change and social comeuppance. Coupled with this is the desire to succeed in school, sports, or the arts. These are just the obvious challenges young people face. The personal trials each person confronts are countless.

You may be able to come up with as many as five private issues that plague you every day. These are your own exclusive disputes that are separate from external factors (like money or work) that you worry about frequently. Certainly, as you age, your concerns may include relationships, finances, career, aging, and your overall health, for example.

Many of these personal issues prompt physicians to encourage some of their IBS patients to seek psychological help. Often, doctors are right to suggest counseling. Your worries may indeed be making you sick! Seeking assistance from a professional equipped to help you deal with some of your emotional concerns is a reasonable conjecture. You may find that speaking to a qualified professional on a regular basis may improve your mental and physical health. Often, spending time with a counselor enables one to learn strategies for coping with their many concerns. Many mental health care providers prescribe antidepressants to those suffering with IBS. After several weeks of treatment patients often find that their symptoms are drastically reduced and their life greatly improved. If your doctor suggests that you consider taking an antidepressive medication, be open to trying several medications before finding one that works best for you. Each one has a slightly different combination of ingredients. You may experience some mild adverse reaction to one type of medication (hyperactivity, for example), while another functions in just the right way. If, after trial and error, a particular antidepressant treatment proves satisfactory in suppressing your symptoms, it can certainly make all the difference in your condition.

A more natural approach to the treatment of IBS can be found with the help of a nutritionist, or by a specialist at your local health food store. Many pharmacies now carry an array of natural herbal supplements and teas suitable in aiding the function of your GI tract, as well as alleviating many of your IBS symptoms. Herbs like chamomile and peppermint have been used to soothe the colon, relax its muscles, and provide relief. These herbs are sold in pill, tea, oil, and capsule form.

Although the more natural remedies are seemingly soothing to your system, they are to be treated as medicine and you must be careful about how you use them. Pregnant women and people on other medications which may interact with herbal remedies should consult a physician before taking any herbal supplements. Even a homeopathic remedy must be consumed with caution.[1]

Some IBS sufferers have found great success with treatment by hypnosis or acupuncture. Though these are unorthodox solutions, many people have found that they are beneficial in controlling stress. Nowadays, it is not uncommon to hear about the success of hypnosis in treating smoking addiction and obesity. Hypnosis has also enabled some IBS sufferers to successfully learn various coping strategies for daily challenges.

Acupuncture, an ancient practice of the Far East, involves inserting hair-thin needles just beneath the surface of the skin into specific target areas of the body. Those who seek this type of treatment find the procedure to be both painless and speedy. Over time, a series of treatments may provide substantial relief from chronic pain by relaxing muscle spasms and regulating the function of the colon. If this route seems appropriate for you, it is certainly worth looking into, but be sure to locate a licensed practitioner of both treatments.

A more common approach to treatment for many IBS sufferers explores various types of meditative exercise, like yoga or Tai Chi. These ancient exercises, developed in India and the Far East, involve rhythmic movement and breathing.

---

[1] *A Note On Chinese Herbs*: Coicis lachyrmajobi, Artemesiae Capillaries, Attractylodis macrocephalae, Codonopsis Pilosulae, and Schisandrae; nearly impossible to pronounce, serve to relax and soothe the muscles of the colon. They also help to alleviate nausea and gas. These herbs can be found in most health food stores. You may also want to find a doctor familiar with Chinese herbology to insure that the correct herbs may be prescribed. Many commonly used herbs and spices may also be beneficial to your health. These include garlic, cinnamon bark, clove, ginger, nutmeg, caraway seed, spearmint, and ginseng. These have been found to improve symptoms like abdominal pain, distension, and diarrhea.

There are several types of yoga that require different levels of exertion. You probably want to begin with a less physically demanding form of yoga, practicing your moves as carefully and as often as possible. The benefits of these meditative exercises are not solely mental and emotional. According to the America Yoga Association, the physical benefits appear to be dramatic as well. Mentally, these exercises encourage you to slow down and relax, if only for the duration of the exercise. The discipline of reducing the pace of your movement and breath could have a very positive impact on your GI tract. By decreasing the flow of adrenaline to the nerves of your colon, you are instantly aiding the natural and proper movement of your digestive organs. Similarly, the movement and rhythmic breathing required for both yoga and Tai Chi actually manipulate the muscles of the colon. This physical manipulation relaxes the muscles of the GI tract over an extended period of time, thereby stimulating the consistent and proper movement necessary for painless digestion. For many sufferers, IBS symptoms are greatly alleviated when exercise becomes part of a daily routine. It is hard to pinpoint the exact reason for this; perhaps exercise strengthens the muscles of the colon too. Whatever the reason may be, try to get moving! It really helps!

Don't feel embarrassed doing these enjoyable exercises. They are accessible to people of all ages and physical abilities and can truly make a positive difference in your life. Be sure to speak with your doctor before beginning any rigorous exercise routine and start with some gentle movements.

The important thing to remember about these courses of treatment is that they approach the "whole being." Though this might sound silly or even "New Age-y," it is important to consider as you become an active participant in improving your health. The notion that your mind and body are connected is a valid argument. That the health of your mind impacts your body, or vice versa, is significant in understanding *how* to take control of your health. Those with IBS who practice behavioral therapies, like psychotherapy and/or relaxation exercises, while receiving more traditional medical care, seem to fare much better in the long run. Ultimately, you cannot ignore your mental health and think that your body will be fine.

Besides stress, there are several other factors that may have a negative impact on your colon and digestion. Lack of sleep, for example, can cause unnecessary stress and dietary problems. When you are not getting adequate rest, all of your bodily functions can become dysfunctional.

Believe it or not, lack of sleep can even contribute to constipation and diarrhea. There are a number of external factors that may contribute to insomnia such as poor relationships, career changes, and money problems. Perhaps these issues require a good deal of attention while you are awake! A consistently good night's sleep will make you feel so much better.

As you explore your own health, hormones, too, are worth considering. Hormonal changes not only influence adolescent sufferers, but affect older adults (particularly women) as well. Pre- and postmenopausal symptoms may last up to ten years! This "change of life" presents its own set of physical changes like hot flashes, headaches, and weight fluctuation. The psychological impact hormonal changes have on women can be just as dramatic. Many women have noticed that their IBS symptoms increase just before or directly after they menstruate. No one is quite sure why hormones influence the digestive process, particularly for women, but the statistics are great. Speak with your physician about the hormone treatments available that may be right for you. The argument over the safety of hormone therapy is varied among medical specialists, so be sure to be fully informed before making a decision.

Once you consider all of the mental and physical factors that may be contributing to your IBS symptoms, begin to think about ways in which you can improve your condition. Ask yourself several questions:

1. **How many** changes can I realistically make?
   Will one major change reduce a particular conflict I experience in my life? Are there several lesser changes I can make that would reduce a constant worry I am troubled by?
2. **What** can I do to reduce stress?
   Can I alter my route to work? Can I find a better job? Should I decide to retire? Do I need to address some important issues with my family/friends?
3. **Which** treatment is right for me?
   Do I take medication? Do I exercise, or both?
4. **Would** I benefit from speaking with a mental health care provider?

Take your time to consider how you often feel during a particularly stressful period. Do you find that your IBS symptoms flare up when you are late to meet someone? Or perhaps when you think about money or relationships? Do you find that you have trouble leaving the bathroom due to a bout of diarrhea when you need to be getting ready for work or school? Perhaps it is constipation you suffer from when you are in unfamiliar surroundings, and your job, unfortunately, requires you to travel a great deal. If it's at all helpful, write down your stress triggers and keep track of how these factors affect your IBS symptoms. The results may surprise you. They may also help to clarify a great deal about your condition. You may find the graph pictured below helpful in evaluating your condition. Chart your triggers for at least two weeks so that you can get an idea of what external factors impact your GI responses. Keep track of your bouts with diarrhea, constipation, bloating and gas, and nausea.

STRESS TRIGGERS AND REFLECTIONS

INCIDENT	WHO I WAS WITH	PHYSICAL REACTION	REFLECTIONS
_____	_____	_____	_____
_____	_____	_____	_____
_____	_____	_____	_____
_____	_____	_____	_____
_____	_____	_____	_____
_____	_____	_____	_____
_____	_____	_____	_____
_____	_____	_____	_____
_____	_____	_____	_____
_____	_____	_____	_____
_____	_____	_____	_____
_____	_____	_____	_____
_____	_____	_____	_____
_____	_____	_____	_____
_____	_____	_____	_____
_____	_____	_____	_____

You may discover that your symptoms are caused by pressure-induced circumstances. You may also find that you respond quite dramatically to situations you thought were fairly benign. Keep a record of the length of your symptoms. IBS symptoms generally last from ten days to two weeks, if not more. Bring this information with you when you visit your doctor and confer with her about your findings.

If your livelihood demands that you maintain a rigorous pace on a daily basis, it may be wise for you to begin a meditative exercise program. Ancient practices like yoga and Tai Chi have made tremendous improvements in the lives of so many IBS sufferers. Others may find that herbal remedies, over-the-counter medication, or antidepressants do the trick. Some may seek relief from a combination of treatments. The important thing to remember is that you can gain greater control over how your body responds to external stimulants and disruptive pressures. And the solutions are as varied and multifaceted as you are!

· six ·

The Food You Eat:
What's Wrong With It?

In addition to the external factors affecting
your GI tract, your diet plays a crucial role in the health of
your digestive organs and the ease with which they function. Any doctor will tell you that the foods you eat are just
as important to good digestion as the way you feel emotionally. Think about your responses to both stress and diet
as you go about making positive changes. You cannot feel
better unless you commit to improving your eating habits.
Once you decide to change your diet you must be commit-
ted! Daunting though it may sound, consistency and dedi-
cation are essential to the prevention of IBS. Once you
decide to take control of what goes into your body, you've
taken a big step. When you develop the habit of choosing
foods that do not overstimulate your colon, you'll see
results. Just imagine enjoying a night out without worrying
about an "accident." Think how much more productive the

day could be without focusing on your painfully distended abdomen. Only you can make the right decision for your body. *You* can be in control. In addition to the suggestions made in chapter 5, dietary changes show the most profound improvements in those suffering with IBS. Understanding which foods trigger your IBS symptoms will make a huge difference in your life!

It is also important to know that changing your diet does not necessarily mean you must make sacrifices. You can still eat some "trigger" foods, but in greater moderation. It is worth taking your time to get in the habit of thinking about what you will eat for your next meal or snack. Envision eating the good foods, not the foods that make you run to the nearest restroom. Picture enjoying a vacation with family or friends free of discomfort and embarrassment. No longer will you have to search desperately for the nearest restroom, or wait for your painful constipation to end. Maybe it's the thought of a terribly bloated abdomen that will get you to reconsider chowing down on that tempting greasy burger and fries.

There is much to learn about what you should avoid and what you can eat, if you have IBS. This chapter will help you gather information about how your food choices can alter your digestion. There are simple dietary alternatives and solutions for much of what ails you.

It is important to remember that, when you overstimulate the colon, you run a great risk of triggering symptoms. The calmer your colon is, the less likely you are to suffer symptoms. Remember: smooth digestion takes place only when the colon is relaxed and its muscles operate in a rhythmic, steady fashion. Consuming foods and beverages that counteract the ability of your colon to function at its optimum level will delay your progress. Some delicious food and beverage suggestions follow later in this chapter.

Finally, make changes in your diet as comfortably as you see fit. Go slowly at first. Don't push yourself too hard. Think about substitutions, or alternative choices, rather than completely eliminating foods you find hard to resist. It may be unrealistic for you to cut out red meat and dairy altogether, so eat less of these items instead. Find alternative choices throughout your day. Instead of eating a cheeseburger and fries for lunch and a steak for dinner, begin with a roast chicken sandwich for lunch and a steak for dinner. Better yet, try roast chicken for lunch and fish for dinner. The steak can be saved for another day.

Keep a **Meal-Response Record**. It will help you track the ways in which the foods you eat affect your health. By recording your dietary intake, you can get both a sense of which foods trigger your symptoms and establish a pattern for the severity and frequency of your pain. The **M-R Record** is important before you begin your IBS prevention program. Keep your record for about two to four weeks. This should allow enough time for you to accurately document the length and severity of each symptom.

MEAL-RESPONSE RECORD

MEAL OR SNACK	PHYSICAL RESPONSE	TIME OF DAY
_____	_____	_____
_____	_____	_____
_____	_____	_____
_____	_____	_____
_____	_____	_____
_____	_____	_____
_____	_____	_____
_____	_____	_____
_____	_____	_____

When we explored digestion in chapter 2, we discussed how it begins in the mouth. When you put food into your mouth, you must chew it slowly and carefully. It is unhealthy to rush through a meal, even when you are in a hurry. Always chew your food so that you are not swallowing large pieces of food and large amounts of air, which contribute to poor and painful digestion.

Avoid chewing gum! It causes you to swallow a lot of air and promotes unnecessary digestion. As you chew gum, particularly on an empty stomach, you send a message to your brain that tells certain receptors you are about to eat. These receptors cannot differentiate between gum chewing and eating a full meal. The GI tract gets the message to begin the digestive process, without the presence of food. The release of acids, combined with the muscular movement of the colon, may then trigger the symptoms of IBS, including gassiness and bloating. Many brands of gum contain sorbitol, a chemical found naturally in some fruit. It's often used as a low calorie sweetener in items like chocolate, jelly, and jam. It can be a major trigger and may cause gas, bloating, and even diarrhea. Don't jeopardize your health for a little stick of gum or a small piece of chocolate.

Alcohol, Tobacco, and Caffeine

IF YOU SMOKE, drink alcohol, or consume lots of coffee (or caffeine-rich beverages) you may experience the symptoms of IBS sooner and more severely. No matter how many times you have heard it, cutting down or abandoning the habits of alcohol, tobacco, and caffeine will make all the difference. Take it one day at a time. Write down your smoking/drinking and/or caffeine consumption in the **Meal-Response Record**. This may help you to control your urges.

Unless you are cooking with alcohol, it is best to stay away from it. When you cook with an alcoholic beverage, the alcohol content actually burns off during the cooking process, leaving only the flavor. Alcohol is a major stimulant and irritant to every organ in your body. When you consume an alcoholic beverage, either with a meal or on an empty stomach, your digestive organs become overstimulated. Overstimulation of the colon can trigger IBS symptoms like gas, bloating, and diarrhea. If in doubt, refrain. You'll be glad you did.

Tobacco may promote stomach diseases such as ulcers and cancer. If you are exposed to secondhand smoke *your* health is also in jeopardy. Remove yourself, if possible, when you find yourself in a smoker's presence.

The stimulant in caffeinated beverages forces the GI tract to overact, which triggers symptoms in IBS sufferers. Perhaps you are one of many people who make a bowel movement after their morning coffee every day. It is more than likely the caffeine in your coffee is prompting your "regularity." Beware of caffeine in other beverages and treats as well, including soda, cocoa, and chocolate. Consider how much caffeine you may be consuming every day. Try substituting with caffeine-free alternatives. If you are going to enjoy an occasional soda, make it a caffeine-free one. Try some of the many herbal teas available at your local market. They're delicious! Herbal teas come in chamomile, peppermint, raspberry, and many other flavors. If herbal teas don't appeal to you, try other flavorful decaffeinated beverages. Brewed or iced, they offer a wonderful alternative to regular coffee and tea and can be found in any grocery or health food store.

Sugar, Fats, and Spices

THIS, TOO, IS a tricky subject. After all, nothing tastes better than fatty, sugary, and spicy food. We love these foods because they're so appealing to our palates. From roasted meats, cheeses, fried chicken, and potatoes, to sumptuous desserts like cake and pie, we are constantly tempted by those scrumptious flavors oozing with unhealthy ingredients like oil and sugar. If you suffer from IBS you may already know that many of these foods can wreak havoc on your digestive system.

Fat, in the form of oils (found in meats like beef, pork, lamb, and veal) and dairy products (milk, cheese) can be major triggers. The process of breaking down fats is especially stressful to the IBS sufferer because it places such a strain on digestion. So try to eliminate as much fat from your diet as possible. Begin by curtailing your red meat intake, particularly if you consume it several times a week. Again, try to think "substitution" rather than "elimination." Cook with nonfat cooking sprays, rather than vegetable oil, and avoid fried foods whenever possible. Fried food is *absolutely no good for you.*

Try eliminating dairy products altogether. Cheese, butter, milk, and ice cream can dramatically trigger your symptoms. Yogurt is the safest dairy food. Its active cultures actually aid in digestion. There are plenty of tasty substitutions when you get dairy urges, such as soy products. Most grocery and health food stores now sell soy-based milk and cheese products and these establishments offer a wide variety of dairy-free substitutes ranging from milk to burgers (in the form of another bean-based product called tempeh). Become familiar with everything your food store has to offer. You might be surprised to find delicious alternatives that won't be harmful to your GI tract and are simple to digest.

Lastly, be wary of the artificial fat Olestra. Olestra is a vegetable oil, sugar-based, calorie-free, fat substitute found in many popular snacks like chips, crackers, cookies, and candies. Olestra acts as a kind of lubricant or diuretic. Since it is not absorbed by the intestine, Olestra quickly travels through your GI tract pushing food at an accelerated pace. Much like a laxative, Olestra promotes bloating, gas, diarrhea, and abdominal discomfort.

Sugar is a tricky substance. Some specialists argue that sugar can trigger symptoms because of the caffeinelike reaction it may induce. Others defend sugar as relatively harmless because it lacks caffeine, alcohol, or fat. Certainly, it is not good for you to consume sugar on a regular basis. It sometimes serves as a stimulant; hence, the desire for a "pick-me-up" sweet treat in the middle of the day. For some IBS sufferers, this stimulant-like effect is a trigger for problems. Remember: Sugar has no health benefits. It is not vitamin- or mineral-rich and, when coupled with fat (contained in countless desserts like cakes, breads, and ice creams), it is just plain unhealthy. With sugar consumption, it is always best to err on the side of caution. Experiment with sugary treats, without the added fat, but don't overdo it. Even if sugar does not trigger you, it is still better to refuse.

How spices affect IBS sufferers varies. Although there is a great range for experimentation with their flavors, spices can be problematic for the IBS sufferer. Again, this is true for some, but not all. Generally, spicy foods that trigger pain, bloating and diarrhea or constipation are coupled with an abundance of fat. Greasy, meat-laden foods like chili, tacos, burritos, and beef patties may be tasty while you eat them, but beware the aftermath. Instead, spice up grilled chicken or fish. Several spicy vegetarian dishes are harmless to your GI tract. Again, experiment with what is right for you. The slightest alteration in your food preparation—from adding spice to omitting fat—can make the difference!

Fiber

UNDERSTANDING FIBER'S ROLE in your diet is very important in gaining control of your condition. When you are suffering from IBS, you need to be especially careful about how much fiber you consume. Too much fiber can be detrimental and one fiber can be better than another.

As previously mentioned, fiber (comprised mainly of plant-based foods) is excreted from your colon at the conclusion of the digestive process. This means that it becomes waste once all prevalent nutrients have been absorbed into the bloodstream. Do not be confused by the fact that, because you excrete fiber (or waste) you do not need it. On the contrary, fiber is essential to maintain the health and regularity of the colon. There are two types of fiber; only one of them is easy to digest.

The "risky" fiber for those with IBS is called insoluble fiber (i.e., it does not dissolve in water). Because it maintains a condensed state in the colon and passes through the GI tract quite quickly, you may be at risk of developing painful bouts of gas, bloating, and diarrhea. Though insoluble fiber is critical in cleansing the colon (thus decreasing the risk of developing more serious colonic conditions like cancer), it needs to be monitored. Too much of this more compacted form of fiber can be aggravating to the IBS sufferer. Try consuming smaller amounts of insoluble fiber throughout the course of a day, rather than large amounts in one sitting.

Not surprisingly, the safer fiber to consume is soluble fiber. This type of fiber can be absorbed and diluted in water, forming a pliable, jelly-like texture that actually pushes waste through the colon until it can be excreted. Because of its nature, it contributes to the proper rhythmic movement of the colon, decreasing the chance of pain, pressure, bloating, gas, diarrhea, and constipation.

If your type of IBS causes regular bouts of constipation, you certainly need to consume more fiber in your diet, but be careful about the *kind* of fiber you consume. If you suffer from diarrhea often, reduce your intake of insoluble fiber and increase your soluble intake.[2] In addition, look for a psyllium supplement (made from psyllium seed, originally from Southeast Asia) in your pharmacy. This grain is high in soluble fiber and is beneficial in treating both constipation *and* diarrhea.

SOLUBLE	INSOLUBLE
Pasta, rice, oatmeal, potatoes, barley, soy, sourdough breads, beans, nuts, lentils	raw fruits and vegetables seeds, sprouts, whole wheat, bran

Whenever you decide to eat something rich in insoluble fiber, consider cooking it beforehand. This will make your meal easily digestible. Steaming, baking, roasting, and grilling fruits and vegetables are good ways to avoid threatening insoluble fiber.

Water

WATER IS CRUCIAL if you suffer from IBS. Even if you don't have this problem, you should be aware of how vital water is to

---

[2] Again, check your condition with your physician before going about treatment.

your health. If you are living with IBS, you must make water your primary beverage. You should consume at least six glasses of water daily. The more the better! Water helps your GI tract to function easily and regularly. In addition, it consistently cleanses the colon, as well as all other organs in the body. If you find that plain water is not exciting enough for you, try adding a squeeze of lemon or lime, flavored ice cubes, or a sprig of mint. There are several decaffeinated, non-carbonated drinks available in the supermarket that are good substitutes as well. Do not use these beverages, however, to replace every glass of water. Just drink, drink, and keep drinking your water!

Now that you are familiar with *what* foods you may eat, start to think about *when* you can eat them. If you have IBS, it is a good idea to develop the habit of leaving home each day with healthy snacks in your bag. As an IBS sufferer, you should never go hungry for long, as doing so will almost always affect your daily routine. Severe hunger will tempt you into making poor dietary choices, like fast foods. You may hurriedly buy a pack of gum, intending to curtail your hunger, while you are in fact triggering an attack. Choose snacks that are convenient to carry and safe to eat, and will travel well. You will be thankful for your decision. It will spare you the agony of having to search for a restroom or suffering with days of painful bloating, gas, or constipation.

If you decide to change anything at all about your diet, first consider the frequency at which you eat. Try to eat smaller, well-combined meals several times a day.

Finally, become a smart shopper. When you have time, explore your grocery store or health food market. Read the labels to familiarize yourself with ingredients, and the fat and sugar content of your favorite and most regularly eaten foods. Try something new! Experiment with healthier alternatives. Have soy burgers instead of burgers made from meat, drink herbal teas instead of soda, and so on. Most of all, enjoy the exploration. There are so many foods available out there. Take advantage of these choices, and get well!

· seven ·

Eating for Good Health

Altering your eating habits is not as hard as you think. There are so many foods and ingredients we know nothing about. This isn't a bad thing; it is simply a result of our complicated lives and busy routines. We all grow up with certain foods; thus we develop the habit of eating the same things every day. If you are suffering from IBS, you may be forced to make adaptations to your diet. The thought of changing your eating habits can be more frightening than living with discomfort. There is no reason to be fearful. You have access to so many tasty and exciting foods and flavors. What's more important, these foods and flavorings will not hurt you! You will not have to struggle with constipation, nor will you need to search desperately for the nearest, most private bathroom. Isn't it worth it to try new foods if it means your health will improve? Having control over pain, bloating, and embarrassment is liberating. So give it a try!

As wonderful as the typical American diet is, there is room for improvement. You are what you eat and poor eating will make you feel poor. Unfortunately, so many of us are inhibited about trying new things because we don't know how to prepare them, or how to incorporate them into the foods that we are already familiar with. Some of the myths and questions about foods and additives you've heard before will be explored here. Use this guide as a reference. Consider it a handy tool as you go about adapting your kitchen and your preparation of food to your new program. Write down the foods that you are most curious about and look for them the next time you visit your favorite food store. You may be surprised to find that a strange-sounding name is actually a commonly used ingredient.

The key to success is to try. Don't be timid. If you have a special recipe from a loved one, add a sprinkle of something here or a dash of something there and ... voilà! You've created a whole new spin on an old favorite!

The correct preparation of food is critical to the success of your new program. Experiment with the recipes on the following pages. They're sure to surprise and delight you. Remember: take your time and get comfortable with substitutions. The smallest step will make a difference. Think about ways in which you can personalize your favorite recipes. Try cooking oil spray instead of vegetable oil, baking rather than frying. Start by changing just one meal a day; work your way up to two and, finally, three. **Don't forget about snacks!** If you suffer from IBS, you cannot risk triggering your symptoms by neglecting to eat. Make it a habit to leave the house with a baggie or Tupperware filled with healthy snacks that will curb your hunger and keep your colon calm. Begin to cut down on your intake of symptom-inducing caffeinated beverages like soda and coffee. Instead, choose herbal teas as your beverage of choice. Flavors like peppermint, fennel, chamomile, rosemary, valerian, and ginger root all function as anti-spasmodic remedies, soothing and relaxing the GI tract. In addition, these herbs help to relieve abdominal cramping, distention, and nausea. Fennel is particularly good for curbing flatulence. Peppermint oil can also be found in capsule form. Follow given directions when taking capsules. The teas may be served warm or iced. Remember to **avoid alcohol!** And if you are pregnant, nursing, or taking medication for any other condition, be sure to share your desire to use these herbs with your doctor before doing so.

Further, try to eliminate as many fats as possible. It's a good idea to get in the habit of cooking with nonfat cooking oil sprays. These come in various flavors from garlic to olive oil and may be used in place of butter and other oils. Along with nonfat cooking spray, begin to use nonstick cookware, if you are not already doing so. Though they may require a little extra care, nonstick pots and pans will make a tremendous difference in your preparation of healthier foods by enabling you to cook without excess oil.

Take the time to educate yourself about food and have fun preparing old favorites in a new and exciting way. Experiment with items that may not be so familiar to you like tofu and tempeh. These two items can be found in any health food market and in many grocery stores. Tofu ranges in texture from silky soft to firm, and can be prepared either raw or cooked in a variety of ways. It's often a good idea when cooking tofu to marinate it in your favorite seasoning for at least twenty minutes. Otherwise it will taste rather bland. Tofu, like a sponge, absorbs any flavor you add to it. Tempeh, also derived from the soybean, is heartier and often available in your grocer's freezer section in pre-marinated patties. Substitute tempeh in ordinarily meat-flavored dishes, like stews, sauces, and burgers. Again, don't be shy about seasoning it up!

Look for low-sodium versions of spices and condiments if sodium intake is of concern for you. In addition to the basic type of soy sauce, for example, Thai thin, mushroom, and sweet black soy sauce are available in any well-stocked

Asian market. Use lemon juice, mustards, honey, wine, syrups, and vinegars for marinades and sauces as well. Lemongrass is used frequently in Asian-inspired dishes. It provides a light, lemony aroma with a hint of sweetness. Mince it and sprinkle on foods as you see fit. There's also Umeboshi Plums, which are plums pickled in brine. Their salty, sour flavor is a great addition to spreads and dressings. Fish sauces, nut butters, and an abundance of flavored soy pastes, sauces, and vinegars enhance a number of foods. In addition, black bean garlic sauce, available in Asian markets and most health food stores, is used in several Asian-inspired dishes. Just a small amount adds lots of aroma and a pungent flavor without heat.

Add several kinds of nuts and seeds to your favorite foods, and carry a bag around for snacking. Try them toasted over cooked vegetables or crushed and sprinkled over baked fruits. There are so many types to choose from! Brazil nuts, macadamia, walnuts, almonds, pecans, and sesame seeds, to name a few. Nuts and seeds provide a healthy, sweet, and textured addition to any meal. Don't be shy! Try variations on flavors that interest you.

Consider cooking with beans like adzuki, cannelloni, fava, and split peas in some of your commonly prepared meals. Instead of long-grain white rice as a side dish, try other grains like kalijira, kasha, quinoa, or millet. These grains offer a range of texture and flavor and are sure to become new favorites. Rather than corn or carrots, try wax beans, bok choy, daikon, leeks, and the many squash varieties. Just remember to cook them first!

A note to parents: As discussed in chapter 8, children may suffer from IBS as well. Whether they do or not, use your condition to teach your child better and healthier eating habits. Invite them into the kitchen with you and have fun! Experiment with each recipe, as you and your child see fit. Healthy foods are not only delicious to eat, they are a joy to prepare. All of the following recipes may be enjoyed by adults and children alike, but there are several that children may become particularly fond of. In addition, there are several adaptations of old favorites, from pancakes to fried chicken to chocolate chip cookies!

The abovementioned ingredients are not original, but they may seem new to you if you haven't prepared food with them before. Begin cooking with those flavors that appeal to you. When you feel daring, include some additions. All the foods listed here are safe if you suffer from IBS. Most importantly, these flavors are proof that eating for IBS sufferers need not be boring!

recipes[3]

---

[3] The recipes offered here have been compiled because they adhere to criteria that are most suitable to IBS sufferers. They are safe for IBS sufferers to eat because they are low in fat and are prepared in ways that avoid triggering symptoms. These recipes are not fried, use minimal amounts of safe oils, and avoid dairy, although you may choose to use dairy, if it is not a problem for you.

▪ drinks ▪

whipped varieties

Yogurt-Banana Milkshake

Serves 2

YOU WILL NEED:

6 oz. soy milk

1 banana

ice cubes

3 tbsp. soy yogurt (flavor of your choice, but vanilla is delicious!)

1 tbsp. maple syrup

Place ingredients in a blender and blend on high until smooth.

Blueberry Smoothie

Serves 2

YOU WILL NEED:

2 bananas, sliced

1 c. blueberries, fresh or frozen

3 tbsp. honey

1 c. soy milk

1 c. ice, optional

Place all ingredients in a blender and blend on high until smooth.

Berry-Soy Smoothie
Serves 2

YOU WILL NEED:
4 oz. silken tofu

6 oz. fruit of your choice: raspberries, mango, blueberries

1 c. ice cubes

2 tbsp. honey

Place all ingredients in a blender and blend on high until smooth.

Berry-Banana Smoothie
Serves 2

YOU WILL NEED:
²/₃ c. vanilla flavored soy milk

1 large banana

1 tbsp. honey

1 ¹/₂ c. strawberries, fresh or frozen

Place all ingredients in a blender and blend until smooth.

Mixed Fruit Smoothie
Serves 2

YOU WILL NEED:
$^1/_2$ mango, sliced

2 c. orange juice

6 strawberries, fresh or frozen

Place all ingredients in a blender and blend until smooth.

Indian Mango Shake
Serves 8

YOU WILL NEED:
2 c. ice cubes

1 c. plain soy milk yogurt

$^1/_4$ c. plus 2 tbsp. fresh lime juice

3 lbs. ripe mangos (peeled, pitted, and cut into chunks)

Place mango chunks into a blender and puree until smooth; you should have about $3^1/_2$ c. Add remaining ingredients (add ice cubes in batches) and blend on high, until smooth.

fruit teas and juices

Melon-Ginger Juice
Serves 6

YOU WILL NEED:
1 c. ginger syrup (recipe follows)
4 lbs. watermelon flesh (seeds removed)
1 c. fresh lime juice

Place watermelon in a juicer and juice about 3 c.

Place watermelon juice in a pitcher and add lime juice and ginger syrup; stir well and serve over ice.

Ginger Syrup
Yields 4 Cups

YOU WILL NEED:
1 piece (about 6 inches) fresh ginger (peeled and thinly sliced)
1¾ c. sugar or Sucanat[4]

Place sugar, ginger, and 3½ c. water in a saucepan. Bring to a boil and cook until sugar dissolves, about 1 minute. Simmer over low heat for another five minutes. Remove from heat and let sit, about 30 minutes. Discard extra ginger slices and store in a Tupperware container, refrigerated for up to two months.

---

[4]A perfect substitute for sugar, this sweetener is made from evaporated whole cane juice, allowing the sweetness of the molasses to remain.

Sweet and Tangy Juice
Serves 2

YOU WILL NEED:
I lime, juiced
4 tsp. honey
3 c. cranberry juice

Stir all ingredients together well, making sure to dissolve honey.

Kiwi-Melon Cooler
Serves 6

YOU WILL NEED:
I c. simple syrup (recipe follows)
I honeydew melon (seeded, rind removed)
$\frac{3}{4}$ c. lime juice
3 kiwis, peeled

Place melon in a juicer and juice about $1\frac{3}{4}$ c.

In a food processor, puree kiwi fruit; you should end up with $1\frac{1}{2}$ c. liquid.

Place both fruit juices in a pitcher and stir in: lime juice, simple syrup and $1\frac{1}{2}$ c. cold water.

Simple Syrup
Yields 6 Cups

YOU WILL NEED:
2¼ c. sugar or Sucanat

Place sugar in a large saucepan and add 4¾ c. water. Bring to a boil and cook until sugar dissolves, about 10 minutes. Remove from heat, place in a Tupperware container and store refrigerated for up to two months.

Blue-Lemon Mint Juice
Serves 6

YOU WILL NEED:
1½ c. mint syrup (recipe follows)
1 pint blueberries, rinsed clean
¾ c. plus 2 tbsp. fresh lemon juice

In a food processor, puree lemon juice and blueberries together. Drain through a fine sieve and discard remaining pulp.

Place juice in a pitcher and add 2 c. cold water and mint syrup. Serve over ice.

Mint Syrup

Yields 3 Cups

YOU WILL NEED:

2 bunches fresh mint, roughly chopped

1 c. sugar or Sucanat

Place ingredients in a large saucepan and add 2¾ c. water. Bring to a boil and cook until sugar dissolves, about one minute. Remove from heat and let sit for 30 minutes. Drain through a fine sieve, discarding mint leaves, and store in a Tupperware container, refrigerated for up to two months.

Jasmine Fruit Tea

Serves 2

YOU WILL NEED:

1 tsp. rosewater[5]

½ tsp. orange flower water

2 tsp. jasmine tea

8 3-oz. cups water

Brew jasmine tea for about 30–60 seconds. Add flavored waters and serve hot, or chilled.

---

[5]Both orange and rose flower waters add a hint of flavor and aroma to baked goods and beverages. Commonly used in Indian and Middle Eastern foods, these are available at Indian markets and pastry supply stores.

Peach Lemonade
Serves 4

YOU WILL NEED:

4 cups peach slices, fresh or frozen

½ c. fresh lemon juice

½ c. water

⅓ c. granulated sugar or Sucanat

Place all ingredients, except peaches, in a blender and mix. Place handfuls of peaches at a time into the blender and puree until all peaches are well blended.

herb teas

Sweet Green Tea
Serves 2

YOU WILL NEED:

2 tsp. honey

2 c. water

¼ tsp. Chinese green tea, powdered

Heat water, but do not bring to a boil. Whisk in powdered tea and honey, until foamy. Serve hot.

Minty Green Tea
Serves 3

YOU WILL NEED:

¾ tsp. green tea, powdered

¼ c. granulated sugar or Sucanat

1 c. fresh mint leaves, packed

3 c. boiling water

In a saucepan, place all ingredients, except tea, over high heat, constantly stirring to dissolve sugar. Lower heat and let steep 5 minutes. Add tea to liquid and steep another minute. Stir to combine before straining mint from liquid. Serve hot or cold, with fresh mint for garnish, if desired.

Lemony Ginger Tea
Serves 3

YOU WILL NEED:

½ c. fresh lemon juice

¼ c. honey

zest of one lemon

¼ c. granulated sugar or Sucanat

3 c. water

1 8-inch piece ginger root, peeled and thinly sliced

In a small saucepan, bring all ingredients, except lemon juice, to a boil. Stir constantly so that sugar dissolves. Remove from heat and cover. Allow to steep ½ hour. Stir in lemon juice and strain. May be served hot or chilled.

▪ soups ▪[6]

Vegetable Stock
Makes about 12 cups

YOU WILL NEED:

3 onions, diced

$1/2$ lb. mushrooms

4 carrots, washed and diced

I rib of celery, washed and chopped

5 garlic cloves

I bunch fresh basil

I bunch fresh thyme

3 springs fresh rosemary

I bunch fresh flat leaf parsley

2 bay leaves (remove before serving)

$3/4$ tsp. salt[7]

$1/2$ tsp. peppercorns

2 c. of any assorted vegetables you may have in your refrigerator

In a large stockpot, over high heat, bring 10 cups of water and all ingredients to a boil. Reduce heat to low and simmer for about 45 minutes. Turn off heat and let stock remain for another 20–30 minutes. Strain and let cool before storing in refrigerator or freezer for up to three months.

---

[6]SOUPS. Indigenous to Mexico, pepitas are green pumpkin seeds; flavor is heightened when toasted, and grinding them makes a wonderful powder; adds a hearty, earthy flavor to sauces, stews, and soups; can be found in health food stores, Latin markets and gourmet markets.

[7]BRAGG LIQUID AMINO is a terrific substitute for salt; made from soy and although similar in texture to soy sauce, it is not as pungent or salty.

Mushroom Soup
Serves 6

YOU WILL NEED:

4 c. vegetable stock

1 lb. mixed mushrooms like oyster, cremini, and shiitake, chopped

2 tbsp. olive oil

1 onion, chopped

3 garlic cloves, minced

$^1/_2$ tsp. kosher salt

$^1/_3$ c. brown rice

2 tbsp. fresh thyme, chopped

$^1/_4$ tsp. white pepper, ground

Bring 1 cup water to a boil in a medium saucepan. Stir in rice and bring to a boil. Cover, reduce heat to low and simmer until tender, about 25–30 minutes. Drain and set aside.

Heat olive oil over medium-high heat in large pot. Place thyme, onion and garlic in oil and sauté, about 2–3 minutes. Reduce heat to medium and add mushrooms, sauté until onions are tender, about 8 minutes. Add stock and bring to a boil. Reduce heat and cover. Let simmer for 25 minutes.

Place half of soup in a blender and puree. Return to pot and add rice. Cover and let simmer for an additional 15 minutes. Season with additional salt and pepper, to taste.

Squash Soup
Serves 8–10

YOU WILL NEED:

1 medium squash, spaghetti or butternut (or any other to
your liking), peeled and cubed

4 garlic cloves, minced

$1/2$ c. green lentils

$1/2$ c. red lentils

1 medium onion, diced

4 c. water

4 c. vegetable stock

3 tbsp. olive oil (or cooking oil spray, olive oil flavored)

$1/2$ c. celery, minced

1–3 tbsp. red wine vinegar, to taste

3–4 medium tomatoes, skinned and diced

$1/2$ tsp. mild curry

$1/4$ c. fresh flat leaf parsley

$1/2$ tsp. coriander

salt and pepper, to taste

Sauté squash in 2 tbsp. olive oil, over medium heat, until just caramelized.

In a separate pan, sauté onion over medium heat in 1 tbsp. olive oil.

In a large pot, add water, stock, celery, and lentils. Over low heat, cook until lentils are tender, about 15 minutes. Add squash, garlic, curry, coriander, and onion. Cook for another 15 minutes and add parsley and tomatoes. Cook for another 5–10 minutes and add red wine vinegar, salt, and pepper, to taste. Simmer another 5–10 minutes before serving.

Black Bean Soup
Serves 10–12

YOU WILL NEED:
8 c. vegetable stock or water
2½ tsp. chili powder
4 garlic cloves, mashed
I quarter-sized slice fresh ginger
I small red onion, chopped
2 carrots, diced
2 tsp. cumin
4 15-oz. cans black beans

Place all ingredients in a large stockpot and bring to a boil. Reduce heat to low and leave pot lid slightly cracked, for 2–4 hours, depending on desired thickness.

Garnish and serve with any of the following:

FRESH CILANTRO, CHOPPED

SCALLIONS, MINCED

SOY SOUR CREAM

FRESH OREGANO, CHOPPED

Sweet Potato Soup
Serves 8

YOU WILL NEED:
2 tsp. honey

2 tsp. maple syrup

1 c. onion, diced

4 garlic cloves, minced

6 c. vegetable stock

1 tsp. dried thyme

2 tsp. canola oil

4 carrots, peeled and diced

1 ½ lbs. (about 3 medium) sweet potatoes, peeled and diced

1–3 tsp. chipotle powder[8], to taste

Place stock, potatoes, thyme, and carrots in a large stockpot and bring to a boil. Cook until vegetables fall apart and mash remaining chunks with a potato masher, if necessary.

Over low-medium heat, sauté onion and garlic in a nonstick skillet, until onions become golden brown. Add to broth chipotle powder, honey, and syrup along with onion and garlic. Mix well and serve with chopped fresh cilantro garnish.

---

[8]CHIPOTLE PEPPERS, found in gourmet markets, health food stores, and Latin groceries; used sparingly, these dried jalapeños pack a lot of punch, but without too much heat; may be stored whole in glass jars, then moistened and chopped or ground finely and used in powder form.

Lentil-Escarole Soup
Serves 4

YOU WILL NEED:

2 cans whole tomatoes, drained, seeded, and chopped

1 bay leaf (remove before serving)

1 garlic clove, minced

1 carrot, chopped

1 $\frac{1}{2}$ tsp. salt

$\frac{1}{4}$ c. green lentils

$\frac{1}{2}$ head escarole, cut into strips

$\frac{1}{8}$ tsp. fresh ground pepper

2 slices French baguette, cubed

2 tsp. olive oil

1 tbsp. soy butter

Melt butter in a stockpot over medium heat. Add garlic and onion and sauté about 5 minutes, until tender. Add: 5$\frac{1}{2}$ c. water, salt, pepper, lentils, tomatoes, and bay leaf and bring to a boil. Lower heat and simmer about 45 minutes until beans are tender.

Preheat oven to 425 degrees. Place bread cubes on a baking sheet and toast until golden, turning periodically.

Place escarole into stockpot and let simmer an additional 5 minutes. Add olive oil and stir. Serve with toasted croutons for garnish.

❖

Miso[9]-Mushroom Soup
Serves 4

YOU WILL NEED:
2 tbsp. miso
1 4-inch square dried kombu[10] (gently use a damp cloth to clean)
2 scallions, minced
²⁄₃ c. fish flakes (Bonito flakes)
¹⁄₃ lb. enoki mushrooms

Place 4 cups of water and kombu in a large saucepan and bring to a boil. Remove kombu and discard. Remove pot from heat and add fish flakes; they will settle to the bottom of the pot. When flakes have settled, strain broth through a fine sieve and discard flakes.

Place broth back in saucepan over medium heat and add mushrooms. Cook until mushrooms soften. Remove about one cup of the broth and place in a bowl. Dissolve miso in this cup and then return to the saucepan, stirring to combine. Garnish serving bowls with scallions before serving.

[9]MISO, found in health food stores, Asian markets, and many large grocery stores; a fermented soybean product available in several forms, adds a salty flavor to foods.

[10]KOMBU is a seaweed used often in Japanese dishes. It is similar to a piece of spinach when cooked, but has a salty, heartier flavor.

Green Pea Soup
Serves 8

YOU WILL NEED:
$\frac{1}{2}$ c. brown rice
4 c. dried split peas
1$\frac{1}{2}$ celery stalks, finely diced
3$\frac{1}{2}$ c. onion, finely chopped
2 c. chopped broccoli
1 tsp. salt
1 tbsp. chopped garlic
2 tbsp. tamari soy sauce[11]
$\frac{1}{2}$ tsp dried thyme
15$\frac{1}{2}$ c. water

Bring $\frac{1}{2}$ c. water to a boil, in a large pot, and add onions. Cook until soft. Add 15 cups of water and the remaining ingredients. Return to a boil. Reduce heat and simmer for 1$\frac{1}{2}$ to 2 hours.

[11]TAMARI. A sweet-and-sour-flavored soy sauce, found in large grocery stores, health food markets, and Asian markets. Also, by using SHOYU. A different soy sauce, made of fermented soy bean, cracked wheat, and sea salt; very flavorful, salty, and aromatic; terrific in soups, spreads, and over cooked vegetables.

Autumn Pumpkin Soup
Serves 6

YOU WILL NEED:
1 16-oz. can of pumpkin flesh
6 c. vegetable or low-sodium chicken broth
1 c. soy cream
3 carrots, sliced
$\frac{1}{2}$ tsp. ground nutmeg
3 celery stalks, sliced
1 tbsp. honey
1 onion, chopped
1 bay leaf (remove before serving)
Salt and pepper, to taste

In a large pot combine carrots, onion, celery, bay leaf, broth, and pumpkin. Bring to a boil. Cover, lower heat, and let simmer for 30 minutes. Remove from heat and place contents in a blender or processor to puree. Return to pot and add remaining ingredients. To increase consistency, add additional soy cream.

▪ snacks ▪

Bruschetta

Serves 2

YOU WILL NEED:
2 6-inch baguettes,[12] sliced lengthwise
2 tsp. olive oil (or cooking oil spray, olive oil flavored)
2 garlic cloves, thinly sliced
1 bunch fresh chives, minced
1 bunch fresh oregano, minced
2 tbsp. fresh basil, finely sliced
1 large tomato, seeded and diced
1 c. soy mozzarella, shredded (optional)

In a small bowl, combine olive oil and garlic. In a separate bowl, combine herbs and tomato. Brush baguette slices with olive oil spread and sprinkle with herbs and tomato (and soy cheese if desired). Grill or toast in an oven at 350 degrees until bread is golden brown and crisp and/or cheese is melted.

[12]French and sourdough breads are best, because they are safe to the GI tract, flavorful and hearty. Use these breads for sandwiches, French toast, bread puddings, etc. Don't throw bread out. Make croutons and bread crumbs from the stale loaf. Stock up when you go shopping and freeze what you don't finish. Leftovers come in handy!

Tasty Tomato, Basil, and Cheese
Serves 6–8

YOU WILL NEED:
6 large, ripe tomatoes, sliced
1 lb. soy mozzarella, or lowfat mozzarella
$\frac{1}{4}$ c. olive oil
1 bunch of fresh basil, rinsed, dried and thinly sliced
1 bunch fresh oregano, rinsed, dried and thinly sliced
1 bunch fresh chives, rinsed, dried and thinly sliced
salt and pepper, to taste

Place tomato slices on a platter. Top with cheese, herbs, salt, and pepper. Drizzle olive oil across tomatoes and serve.

For a meal alternative: place tomatoes and accompaniments in between two slices of lightly toasted, hearty, French or sourdough bread. Try brushing the outside of the bread with olive oil and grilling—it's a new take on an old favorite—grilled cheese!

▪ dips and spreads ▪

Tomato-Cilantro Salsa
Serves 4

YOU WILL NEED:

1 bunch fresh cilantro, chopped

1 small, sweet white onion, diced

1 lime, juiced, plus additional, if desired

2 large tomatoes, diced

salt and pepper, to taste

Combine all ingredients and add additional lime juice, to taste. Serve chilled or at room temperature.

Eggplant Hummus
Serves 6–8

YOU WILL NEED:

1 c. canned chickpeas (garbanzo beans), rinsed and drained

2 tbsp. tahini[13]

1 garlic clove, mashed

1/4 c. fresh lemon juice

1 tbsp. fresh flat leaf parsley, chopped

1/4 tsp. kosher salt

1 medium eggplant, peeled and quartered

Steam eggplant over a double boiler until tender, about 45 minutes. Let eggplant cool before placing into a blender (cut flesh into smaller pieces, if necessary). Add remaining ingredients, except parsley and puree until smooth (no lumps should remain). Transfer hummus puree into a serving bowl and garnish with parsley before serving.

---

[13]TAHINI: this tasty paste made from sesame seeds makes a terrific sandwich spread; found in health food markets and large grocery stores.

Refried Bean Spread
Serves 4

YOU WILL NEED:
2 c. water

1 tsp. chili powder

2 tbsp. olive oil (or cooking oil spray, olive oil flavored)

1 tsp. garlic salt

1 c. onion, diced

1 garlic clove, minced

1 tbsp. lime juice, fresh

1 c. red lentils, rinsed and drained

2 tbsp. fresh cilantro, thinly sliced

In a medium saucepan over medium-high heat, combine garlic salt, chili powder, water, and lentils. Bring to a boil. Reduce heat and cook until lentils are smooth and creamy, about 40–45 minutes.

In a separate pan, heat olive oil and sauté onion until faintly colored. Add garlic, being careful not to let garlic burn. Add cooked lentils to oil and garlic and cook together, about 5 minutes. Remove from heat and stir in lime juice. Garnish with cilantro and serve with baked chips or crackers.

White Fish Bean Dip
Serves 6–8

YOU WILL NEED:

1 c. smoked white fish, skin and bones removed

1 16-oz. can of white beans, rinsed and drained

1 tbsp. olive oil (or cooking oil spray, olive oil flavored)

¼ c. soy milk

1 lemon, juiced

1 garlic clove, minced

1 tsp. dried oregano

1 tsp. dried dill

¼ tsp. white pepper

2 tsp. dried basil

salt and pepper, to taste

Puree all ingredients together in a blender or food processor, until smooth. Chill before serving.

Black Bean Dip
Serves 4

YOU WILL NEED:

3 cloves, minced to a paste

¼ tsp. chipotle pepper, ground (add more for increased heat)

2 tsp. chili powder garlic

2 tbsp. soy cream cheese

1 tbsp. lime juice

1 tbsp. white wine vinegar

1 15-oz. can black beans, rinsed and drained

Puree all ingredients together in a blender or food processor until smooth. Serve warm with baked chips, on a baguette or with crackers: may be microwaved, on high, 3–5 minutes.

Cannellini Dip

Serves 6–10

YOU WILL NEED:
1 tbsp. minced garlic

1 tbsp. white wine vinegar[14]

1 tbsp. dried bread crumbs

$1/2$ tsp. fresh ground pepper

$1/2$ tsp. kosher salt

2 15-oz. cans cannelloni beans, drained, reserve liquid

1 tsp. plus 2 tbsp. olive oil

1 onion, minced

2 tsp. fresh rosemary, minced

1 tbsp. fresh, grated soy parmesan cheese

Preheat oven to 350 degrees.

In a saucepan, heat 1 tbsp. oil over medium heat. Sauté onion and garlic until translucent. Add rosemary, beans, salt, and pepper. Cook for about 5 minutes.

Place beans in a food processor and add vinegar, 1 tbsp. oil, and 3 tbsp. reserved bean liquid. Puree until smooth.

In a separate bowl, add bread crumbs, cheese, remaining rosemary, and remaining oil. Combine well.

In an oven-safe bowl, add bean puree and top with breadcrumb mixture. Bake until browned, about 20 minutes.

---

[14]VINEGARS: There are so many flavors to choose from these days, in addition to the commonly used red or white wine and balsamic varieties. Adding vinegar to foods during the cooking process decreases its acidity in many varieties.

Northern Bean Dip
Serves 8–10

YOU WILL NEED:
2 cans white beans, rinsed and drained
$^1/_2$ tsp. vegetable bouillon
1 garlic clove
6–8 chives
4 sprigs rosemary, leaves only
1 tbsp. olive oil (or cooking spray, olive oil flavored)
$^1/_2$ tsp. salt

In a blender or food processor, puree all ingredients together until smooth.

Green Olive Spread
Yields about 1 Cup

YOU WILL NEED:
3 tbsp. capers, drained
1 garlic clove, peeled
2 tsp. fresh lemon juice
5 anchovy fillets
1 c. pitted green olives
salt and pepper, to taste

Place all ingredients in a food processor and grind until a smooth paste forms.

Guacamole
Serves 2–4

YOU WILL NEED:

1 tbsp. fresh cilantro, chopped, plus extra for garnish

1 garlic clove, minced

¼ c. white onion, diced

1 small lime, juiced

1 large Hass avocado, peeled and diced

chili powder, to taste, optional

1 ripe plum tomato, diced (optional)

salt and pepper, to taste

In a large bowl, blend all ingredients together with a fork until well combined. Garnish with cilantro before serving at room temperature.

Pumpkin-Bean Dip
Serves 8–10

YOU WILL NEED:

1 15-oz. can chickpeas (garbanzo beans), drained and rinsed
1 15-oz. can pumpkin flesh
1 tsp. whole mustard seeds, toasted
1 tsp. kosher salt
2 tbsp. fresh lemon juice
2 tbsp. olive oil
1 tsp. cumin seeds, toasted
1 tsp. whole coriander seeds, toasted
$\frac{1}{2}$ tsp. fresh ground black pepper
1 tsp. fresh thyme leaves

In a spice grinder, grind all toasted seeds and set aside.

Combine spices with pumpkin flesh, oil, beans, salt, pepper, lemon juice, and thyme in a food processor and blend until smooth.

▪ sides and sauces ▪

potatoes

Candied Yams
Serves 6

YOU WILL NEED:

3 large sweet potatoes, peeled and cubed

1 c. water

2 tbsp. canola oil

1/2 c. brown sugar, packed

pinch of salt

pinch of cayenne, or to taste

In a heavy-bottomed skillet, heat the oil over medium heat. In a separate bowl, mix the salt, cayenne, water, and sugar together. Add potatoes to the skillet and pour in water mixture. Stir. Cook covered for 25 minutes. Turn potatoes and cook, covered, for another 20 minutes. Remove cover and stir potatoes occasionally until fork-tender and well coated with caramelized sugar.

Sage Sweet Potatoes with Pecans

Serves 8

YOU WILL NEED:

1 tbsp. plus 1 tsp. fresh sage, chopped

8 sweet potatoes, pricked several times with a fork

1 1/3 c. soy cottage cheese

1 tbsp. shallots, minced

1/4 c. pecans, chopped

1 1/4 tsp. salt

1/4 tsp. fresh ground pepper

olive oil cooking spray

Preheat oven to 450 degrees. Place sweet potatoes on a baking sheet and bake until tender, about 45 minutes. Remove from oven and let cool. Lower oven to 375 degrees.

Slice sweet potatoes in half and remove and discard the skins from half of them (8 halves). Place skinless potatoes in a bowl and mash. Scoop out the flesh of the remaining potatoes halves, leaving skins intact.

In a saucepan coated with olive oil, add shallots and sauté over medium heat, about five minutes. Add 1 tbsp. sage and sauté another 2 minutes, until fragrant. Remove from heat before adding to a food processor. Add cottage cheese, salt, and pepper to shallots and puree until smooth. Add mashed sweet potatoes and combine well.

Scoop potato mixture into skins and sprinkle with pecans and remaining sage. Place stuffed potatoes in a baking dish and bake about 20 minutes, until nuts are toasted and aromatic.

Crispy Garlic Potatoes
Serves 4

YOU WILL NEED:
6 garlic cloves, minced

1 tsp. garlic salt

1 tbsp. olive oil

2 lbs. small new potatoes, red or white

In a large, nonstick skillet, place potatoes and pour water over them until they are covered. Add garlic, salt, and oil and bring to a boil. Reduce heat to medium and cook potatoes until water evaporates, turning every so often, about 20–25 minutes. Raise heat again to high and cook potatoes, turning often, until they brown and become crunchy, about 15 minutes.

Crispy Baked French Fries
Serves 4

YOU WILL NEED:
5 baking potatoes

$\frac{1}{8}$ c. canola oil, or nonfat cooking spray

salt, to taste

Scrub potatoes and slice, julienne style, like French fries. Preheat oven to 400 degrees. Toss potatoes with oil in a large bowl. Make sure all potato slivers are coated in oil and spread them evenly on a nonstick pan. Sprinkle with salt and bake until crispy on the edges and tender in the center, about 40 minutes.

Sweet Yams with Miso Sauce
Serves 4

YOU WILL NEED:

2 tbsp. mirin[15]

1 tsp. white wine vinegar (or white wine)

2 tbsp. white miso paste

1 tsp. brown sugar

1 tsp. honey

1/4 tsp. toasted sesame oil[16]

2 lbs. sweet potatoes, peeled and cubed

In a double boiler, steam potatoes about 20 minutes, until fork tender. In a separate bowl, mix together remaining ingredients until smooth. Place potatoes in the bowl and gently toss to coat well. Refrigerate to cool until serving.

---

[15]MIRIN. Traditionally used in Japanese cooking; derived from short-grained rice and distilled alcohol, this sweet-flavored sake adds a distinct aroma and flavor to foods, not too unlike a teriyaki sauce, found in health food stores and Asian markets.

[16]SESAME OIL. Just a little bit of this nutty, rich oil goes a long way; can be found in large grocery stores, Asian markets, and health food stores.

Bubblin' Baked Beans
Serves 4

YOU WILL NEED:
1 lb. dried navy beans, soaked in water overnight
2 tsp. dry mustard
1 onion, diced
$\frac{1}{2}$ c. molasses
$\frac{1}{2}$ c. ketchup (sugar free, if possible)
salt and pepper, to taste

Add beans and 2 tsp. of salt to a large pot filled with enough water to cover beans. Cover and turn heat up high, bringing water to a boil. Allow water to boil for a moment before lowering heat to a simmer. Uncover pot slightly and cook beans until tender, about 1 hour. Check periodically to see if more water is needed.

Drain beans when tender and preheat oven to 300 degrees. Combine beans with dry mustard and molasses. In an ovenproof, large pot, place the bean mixture, onion, ketchup, salt, and pepper. Do this slowly as there will be a lot! Bake uncovered for about 3 hours, checking occasionally. You don't want the beans to burn.

Sweet Glazed Carrots
Serves 4

YOU WILL NEED:
3–4 carrots, peeled and sliced
2 tbsp. maple sugar
1 tbsp. soy margarine
½ c. water
1 tsp. cider vinegar
salt and pepper, to taste

Place the carrots in a medium skillet with water. Cook over medium-high heat, covered, until carrots are soft. Add cider vinegar, maple sugar, and margarine. Leave pot uncovered, and sauté over high heat, continuously stirring for about 3 minutes. Season with salt and pepper.

Squirrel's Squash

Serves 4

YOU WILL NEED:

1 large acorn squash, seeds removed and cut into 8 chunks

1 tbsp. soy margarine

1 clove garlic, pressed

1 c. vegetable broth

$^1/_2$–$^3/_4$ tsp. of salt

2$^1/_2$ tsp. honey

1$^1/_2$ tsp. fresh thyme, chopped

Put broth and squash in a large pot and bring to a boil. Lower heat, cover and cook squash until tender, about 20–25 minutes. In a separate small saucepan, sauté garlic in margarine for a couple of minutes; do not burn. Combine garlic/margarine mixture with squash. Mix in remaining ingredients. Stir over low heat for another 5 minutes. Serve.

Gingery Butternut Squash

Serves 4

YOU WILL NEED:

1$^1/_2$ lbs. butternut squash, peeled and diced

1$^1/_2$ tsp. minced ginger

2 tsp. maple syrup

2 tbsp. soy margarine

salt and pepper

Steam squash, covered, in a double boiler until tender, about 20–25 minutes. Place squash in a food processor and add ginger and margarine. Process until smooth.

Edamame
Serves 4

YOU WILL NEED:

I tsp. toasted sesame seeds, slightly ground along with $^1/_2$ tsp. kosher salt

2 c. fresh soybeans, left in the pod or shelled

In a double boiler, steam soybeans until tender, about 5 minutes (a few minutes longer if still in pod). Place beans in a serving dish and sprinkle with ground and salted seeds. Toss to coat.

Roasted Asparagus
Serves 6–8

YOU WILL NEED:

2 bunches thin asparagus, stem ends removed

I tsp. kosher salt

$^1/_2$ tsp. fresh ground black pepper

2 tbsp. olive oil, plus extra for serving

Preheat oven to 425 degrees. Place asparagus evenly in a roasting pan and drizzle with olive oil; season with salt and pepper. Roast in oven until fork tender, about 10 minutes.

Drizzle with a little extra olive oil before serving.

Winter Roasted Vegetables
Serves 6

YOU WILL NEED:

12 oz. brussels sprouts, cleaned and trimmed

1 lb. squash (butternut or acorn), peeled and cubed

4 small turnips, peeled and halved

1 red onion, peeled and quartered

1 rutabaga, peeled and diced

1 yellow or white onion, peeled and quartered

3 carrots, peeled and sliced lengthwise

2 tbsp. olive oil (1 tbsp. per roasting pan)

1 tbsp. fresh rosemary, minced

2 tsp. fresh thyme, minced

1 tsp. salt

$\frac{1}{2}$ tsp. fresh ground pepper

olive oil cooking spray

Preheat oven to 450 degrees. Coat two large roasting pans with cooking oil spray. Arrange vegetables evenly in both pans and drizzle all of them with 1 tbsp. olive oil, tossing gently to coat. Sprinkle salt, pepper, thyme, and rosemary over vegetables and roast for 25 minutes. Turn vegetables for even cooking and roast another 15 minutes, until tender.

Sweet Sautéed Spinach
Serves 4

YOU WILL NEED:

2 bunches fresh spinach, cleaned and stems removed

1/2 c. golden raisins, soaked in warm water and drained

I tbsp. olive oil (or cooking oil spray)

1/4 c. pine nuts

2 garlic cloves, thinly sliced

salt and pepper, to taste

Heat olive oil in a large pot and sauté garlic for about 1 minute. Add nuts and sauté until golden, another minute. Add raisins, spinach, salt, and pepper, to taste. Stir constantly until spinach wilts, about 4 minutes.

Citrus Relish
Yields 2 Cups

YOU WILL NEED:

I c. sugar

3/4 c. fresh orange juice

1/4 c. crystallized ginger, finely chopped

3 c. fresh cranberries

zest of I orange

zest and juice of I lemon

Place 2 cups of the cranberries into a food processor and blend until chopped. In a medium saucepan over medium heat, place sugar, zests, ginger, and orange juice and simmer. Add chopped cranberries and cook about 15 minutes, until thickened. Remove from heat. Add lemon juice and remaining 1 c. berries. Stir to combine and let cool.

Tomato Mango Relish
Serves 6

YOU WILL NEED:

2 small, ripe mangoes, peeled and diced

5 ripe plum tomatoes

$1/4$ c. fresh lime juice, or to taste

2 tbsp. honey, or to taste

1 tsp. ground chipotle pepper, or to taste (optional)

salt and pepper, to taste

In a broiler or on a grill, roast tomatoes until skins blacken and puff, turning frequently for even roasting. Combine tomatoes and remaining ingredients, except mango, in a blender and puree until smooth. Place tomato puree in a bowl and stir in mango. Add additional honey and/or lime juice, to taste.

▪ morning meals ▪

Cornmeal Pancakes
Serves 4

YOU WILL NEED:
$1/2$ c. cornmeal

3 tbsp. granulated sugar or Sucanat

2 tsp. baking powder

I tsp. baking soda

$1/2$ c. soy milk

$1/8$ tsp. salt

I $1/4$ c. plain soy yogurt

$1/2$ stick soy margarine, melted

3 large egg whites[17]

I c. all purpose unbleached white flour

In a medium bowl, whisk together sugar, baking powder, baking soda, flour, cornmeal, salt, and soy milk.

In a separate bowl, combine egg whites and yogurt. Blend with dry ingredients and add melted margarine. Mix well to combine.

Lightly coat and heat a nonstick skillet and pour ladleful portions of batter onto the skillet. Let batter cook, undisturbed, until bubbles form and burst and edges turn a golden brown, about 3 minutes. Flip pancakes over and cook another 1–2 minutes until golden brown. Serve with warm maple syrup.

For a variation, add banana slices, blueberries, or strawberries.

---

[17]For some IBS sufferers, egg yolks *can* trigger a reaction; egg whites are not a problem. If egg yolks are not a trigger, go ahead and use whole eggs whenever you want. Several of the recipes in chapter 10 (**Your Child and IBS)** call for whole eggs. Many children do not have a reaction to yolks, so feel free to use them in your cooking. Look for organic eggs, which are free of the chemical preservatives that may cause a problem for your GI tract. If egg yolks do trigger a reaction in either you or your child, stop using them at once. Egg substitutions (just egg whites) are available in the dairy section of your grocery store or health food market.

▪ muffins[18] ▪

Melt in Your Mouth Blueberry Muffins
Makes about 18 muffins

YOU WILL NEED:
1 c. blueberries, washed, drained and dried

2 eggs or 4 egg whites

$1/4$ tsp. baking soda

$1/2$ tsp. salt

$2^{1}/_{2}$ tsp. baking powder

1 tsp. ground cinnamon

2 c. unbleached flour

$2/3$ c. Sucanat

1 c. soy or non-fat milk (lactose free, if necessary)

$1/2$ c. soy margarine, plus extra for muffin tins

Preheat oven to 450 degrees. Grease muffin tins with soy margarine.

In a medium bowl, combine dry ingredients. In another bowl, add milk, margarine, and eggs, whisk until smooth. Combine dry and wet ingredients together and stir well. Gently add berries and mix into batter.

Spoon muffin batter into greased tins, leaving a little room at the top for batter to expand and rise. Bake 15–20 minutes. A toothpick should come out clean, not wet and sticky. Allow muffins to cool before removing.

---

[18]NUT BUTTERS are available in delicious, natural flavors like almond, cashew, and macadamia; use as you would peanut butter, in baking, or as a spread. They're wonderful on warm muffins, and toast.

Perfectly Perfect Pumpkin Muffins
Makes about 14 muffins

YOU WILL NEED:

1 16-oz. can of pumpkin flesh

3$\frac{1}{2}$ c. unbleached flour

1 tsp. ground cinnamon

1 tbsp. baking powder

1 tsp. baking soda

1 tsp. salt

3 large eggs

2 tsp. pumpkin pie spice

$\frac{2}{3}$ c. maple sugar

$\frac{2}{3}$ c. soy or non-fat milk (lactose free, if necessary)

$\frac{2}{3}$ c. honey

$\frac{3}{4}$ c. soy margarine—softened, plus extra for muffin tins

Preheat oven to 400 degrees. Grease muffin tins with margarine.

Combine flour, pumpkin pie spice, baking soda, baking powder, and salt. In another bowl, beat eggs and add pumpkin flesh, soy margarine, honey, milk, maple sugar, and ground cinnamon. Combine both wet and dry ingredients.

Spoon batter into greased muffin tins, leaving a little room for batter to expand and rise. Bake 25–30 minutes. A toothpick should come out clean, not wet and sticky. Allow muffins to cool before removing.

Creamy Combo Muffins

Makes about 12 muffins

YOU WILL NEED:

1 c. grain sweetened chocolate chips

1/2 c. roasted peanuts, chopped

2 c. unbleached flour

2/3 c. creamy, all natural peanut butter

1 tbsp. baking powder

1/3 c. Sucanat

1/2 tsp. salt

1 1/3 c. soy or non-fat milk (lactose free, if necessary)

2 eggs or 4 egg whites

1/4 c. soy margarine, melted, plus extra for muffin tins

Preheat oven to 400 degrees. Grease muffin tins with margarine. Combine Sucanat, salt, baking powder, and flour in a large bowl. In another bowl, mix the peanut butter until smooth. Add the milk to the peanut butter and combine well. Mix in margarine and eggs until well blended. Add peanuts and chocolate chips. Mix wet ingredients together with dry ingredients and combine well.

Add batter to muffin tins and bake about 15 minutes. Toothpick should come out clean, not wet and sticky. Allow muffins to cool before removing.

Coffee Crunch Muffins

Makes 12 muffins

YOU WILL NEED:

FOR MUFFINS:

1 tsp. vanilla

$1/2$ tsp. kosher salt

$3^1/2$ tsp. baking powder

2 tsp. cinnamon

$2^1/3$ c. all purpose unbleached white flour

1 c. soy milk

1 egg white, beaten

2 tbsp. soy margarine, softened to room temperature

$1/3$ c. maple sugar

FOR TOPPING:

$1/2$ tsp. cinnamon

$1/2$ c. maple sugar

$1/3$ c. all-purpose unbleached white flour

$1/4$ c. soy margarine

Preheat oven to 375 degrees.

With an electric mixer, cream margarine and maple sugar. Add egg white and blend well.

In a separate bowl, combine baking powder, cinnamon, salt, and flour. Blend in with creamed ingredients and add soy milk. Add vanilla and stir to combine.

Mix together topping ingredients until well blended and crumbly.

Fill 12 muffin tins a little more than halfway with batter and top evenly with crumbly topping. Bake for 25–30 minutes until muffins are nicely browned and toothpick comes out clean.

❖

Mushroom Omelet
Serves 2

YOU WILL NEED:
4 egg whites
$\frac{1}{2}$ c. onion, diced
I c. fresh mushrooms, any type, chopped
I tbsp. fresh parsley
I garlic clove, minced
salt and pepper, to taste

Whisk egg whites in a medium bowl until foamy. Heat a nonstick skillet and coat with cooking oil spray. Pour in eggs and add remaining ingredients on one side of omelet only, leaving half without topping.

Cook omelet a couple of minutes while shaking the skillet gently, until edges turn golden brown. Season to taste with salt and pepper. With a spatula, gently lift the omelet edges on the side *without* vegetables and flip over top of vegetable portion.

Allow omelet to cook another minute before gently sliding onto a serving plate.

Huggable Hash Browns
Serves 4

YOU WILL NEED:
3 tbsp. soy margarine or olive oil
1–1½ pounds russet potatoes, peeled
1 egg or 2 egg whites, beaten
salt and pepper, to taste

In a medium saucepan, cover potatoes with water and bring to a boil. Cook until fork-tender. Remove and drain potatoes. Allow potatoes to cool. When potatoes are cool enough to handle, grate them. Add beaten egg and combine. Shape potato shavings into flattened patties, about the size of your hand (or your child's). Heat a large skillet. Add margarine or oil. Carefully place potato portions into the hot skillet (as many that will fit without touching) and cook until golden brown on both sides. Season with salt and pepper.

For variation add any other vegetable, herbs, and/or grated soy cheese.

hot cereals

Multigrain Flakes with Winter Fruit
Yields approximately 4 Cups

YOU WILL NEED:
$1/2$ c. buckwheat kasha
$1/2$ c. soy flakes
$1/4$ c. hazelnuts, toasted
2 oranges, peeled and segments separated
2 c. apple juice
1 c. cranberries (fresh or frozen)

Place cranberries and 2 tbsp. of water in a medium skillet over medium-high heat. Cook until berries soften and burst, about 2 minutes. Add oranges and stir to combine. Remove from heat.

In another saucepan bring 3 c. of water and apple juice to a boil. Add soy flakes and cook five minutes, covered. Stir in kasha, cover and cook another 10 minutes. Remove cover and cook another five minutes, so that liquid will evaporate. Place cooked grains in serving bowls and add dollops of fruit mixture. Garnish with toasted nuts.

Sugar-Berry Oatmeal
Serves 2

YOU WILL NEED:
2 tsp. brown sugar
$\frac{1}{2}$ c. blueberries, fresh or frozen
2 c. vanilla flavored soy milk
I c. rolled oatmeal (not an instant variety)

Place all ingredients in microwave-safe dish, cover with plastic wrap and microwave for 2 minutes on high. Carefully remove dish from microwave, peel back plastic and stir. Replace plastic wrap and microwave another 1½ minutes until berries burst and oats thicken.

Cozy Oatmeal
Serves 4

YOU WILL NEED:
1½ c. rolled oats
2½ c. water
1½ tbsp. raisins (golden, brown, or a mix of the two)
I tsp. ground cinnamon
½ banana, thinly sliced
2 tbsp. maple syrup

Boil water in a medium-sized pot, add rolled oats and stir. Cook and stir frequently until water is absorbed, remove from heat. Add maple syrup, cinnamon, and raisins. Garnish with banana slices and extra syrup if desired.

french toasts

Cornmeal Toast

Serves 6

YOU WILL NEED:

2 c. stone-ground yellow cornmeal

2 quarts vanilla-flavored soy milk

2 tbsp. soy margarine

$\frac{1}{2}$ c. golden raisins

4 tbsp. maple syrup

In a medium saucepan, bring milk and margarine to a boil. Slowly whisk in cornmeal and continuously stir until cornmeal mixture thickens, about 10 minutes. Add syrup and mix in well before adding raisins. Pour batter into a loaf pan ($8\frac{1}{2}$ x $4\frac{1}{2}$ is a good size) and refrigerate until chilled.

Turn loaf pan upside-down and remove cornmeal loaf. Slice evenly into about 12 slices. Heat a large skillet over medium heat and coat with cooking oil spray. Place as many loaf slices into skillet as will fit without overlapping and cook on either side until golden brown. Serve with warm syrup.

Lemon French Toast
Serves 6

YOU WILL NEED:
2 egg whites
zest of 1 lemon
$\frac{1}{2}$ c. vanilla-flavored soy milk
$\frac{1}{2}$ package (about 12.5 oz. package) silken tofu, drained and patted dry
1 baguette loaf, sliced into 1-inch thick slices

Combine in a blender until smooth: tofu, egg whites, milk, and lemon zest. Pour batter in deep dish and place baguette slices in batter. Allow bread to soak about 10 minutes.

Heat a skillet over medium heat and coat with cooking oil spray. Place as many baguette slices into skillet as will fit without overlapping and cook on either side until golden brown. Serve with warm syrup and garnish with chopped berries of your choice and lemon zest.

▪ main meals ▪

Fish and Seafood[19]

Lemon-Soy Swordfish
Serves 4

YOU WILL NEED:
4 8-oz. swordfish fillets
1/2 tsp. Dijon mustard
2 tbsp. olive oil (or cooking oil spray, olive oil flavored)
1 tbsp. fresh lemon juice
1/4 tsp. lemon zest
1 1/4 tbsp. soy sauce
1/4 tsp. garlic, minced

Rinse fillets in cool water and pat dry. Set aside. Place all remaining ingredients in a blender and blend until emulsified. Pour half of the liquid in a baking pan and reserve the other half in a bowl for basting. Place fillets in baking pan with marinade and let sit for 20 minutes. Broil or grill fillets basting often with reserved marinade.

[19]FISH SAUCE, used most often in Thai recipes; found in Asian groceries, often in health food stores and fish markets; adds a wonderfully light but essential fishy flavor to many dishes.

Swordfish Fillets with Tomatoes and Lentils

Serves 4

YOU WILL NEED:

1 15-oz. can lentils

2 plum tomatoes, chopped

1 tbsp. olive oil, plus 1 tsp. extra virgin olive oil

1 shallot, diced

1 tsp. vermouth

1 garlic clove, minced

4 swordfish fillets, about 6 oz. each

salt and pepper, to taste

Rinse fillets in cool water and pat dry. Season with salt and pepper, to taste and set aside.

In a skillet over medium heat, add 1 tbsp. olive oil and heat. Add garlic and shallot and sauté until fragrant and soft, about 5 minutes. Add vermouth, lentils, and tomatoes and sauté 5–8 minutes. Set aside.

In a separate, large skillet, heat 1 tsp. extra virgin olive oil and when very hot, add the fillets and sear, about 2 minutes per side.

Serve with a heaping spoonful of lentil-tomato mixture.

Dijon-Dill Salmon
Serves 4

YOU WILL NEED:
1 lb. salmon fillet
1/3 c. Dijon mustard
1 tbsp. dill weed
1 tbsp. canola oil
1/4 tbsp. packed brown sugar

Preheat oven to 350 degrees. Rinse salmon in cool water and pat dry.

In a small bowl mix mustard, dill, oil, and brown sugar. Place salmon in a baking dish that has been coated with cooking oil spray. Pour Dijon-dill sauce over salmon, before baking 25–30 minutes. Serve with rice, sweet potatoes, cooked vegetables, and lemon wedges, for garnish.

Japanese Honey Cod
Serves 2

YOU WILL NEED:
cooking oil spray
1 c. honey teriyaki sauce
2 cod fillets

Place the sauce in a large bowl and marinate the fillets at room temperature for 45 minutes.

Coat a skillet with cooking oil spray and heat over high heat. Place the cod in the well-heated skillet and sear until very flaky and golden brown on both sides.

Sun-Dried Tomato Crusted Salmon
Serves 4

YOU WILL NEED:
4 salmon fillets, about 6 oz. each

1 c. bread crumbs, very fine

cooking oil spray, olive oil flavored

¼ c. pitted kalamata olives, finely chopped

¼ c. sun-dried tomatoes, drained and finely chopped

3 garlic cloves

2 tbsp. soy margarine

1 ½ tsp. fresh rosemary

2 tsp. fresh thyme

6 tsp. Dijon mustard

Rinse fillets in cool water and pat dry. Set aside.

In a bowl mix garlic, sun-dried tomatoes, olives, thyme, rosemary, and margarine. Preheat oven to 400 degrees. Add 2 tsp. mustard and bread crumbs and mix well.

Coat a baking dish with cooking oil spray. Place fillets in baking pan and spread a teaspoonful of remaining mustard over each. Spread bread crumb mixture evenly over each fillet and bake about 10–12 minutes.

Southern "Fried" Catfish

Serves 4

YOU WILL NEED:

2 tsp. Cajun seasoning or Old Bay seasoning

1/3 c. yellow cornmeal

1 1/2 lbs. catfish fillets, rinsed and patted dry

2 egg whites, whisked

cooking oil spray

Mix cornmeal and seasoning on a large plate. Dip fillets into egg and shake off excess. Place fillet on cornmeal mixture and coat both sides evenly, shaking off excess. Set aside. Repeat with remaining fillets.

Heat a large skillet coated with cooking oil spray, over medium high heat and place fillets flat in skillet, without overlapping. Cook until golden brown and crunchy on both sides. Garnish with lemon wedges.

❖

Lemon Shrimp Cocktail
Serves 6

YOU WILL NEED:
1 lb. jumbo shrimp, shelled and cleaned

FOR MARINADE:
3 tbsp. white wine vinegar
2 tsp. olive oil
3 tbsp. fresh lemon juice
1 tsp. salt
1 tbsp. water
1 tbsp. granulated sugar

Combine all ingredients, except shrimp, in a bowl. Set aside.

Bring a large pot of water to a boil. Add shrimp and cook until shrimp turn a bright pink, just a few minutes. Drain shrimp and add to bowl of marinade. Toss and let sit, refrigerated for at least 4 hours. Drain shrimp, discarding marinade, and serve with cocktail sauce; recipe follows.

FOR COCKTAIL SAUCE:
3/4 c. ketchup
1/4 c. horseradish
1 lemon, juiced

Combine all ingredients well and serve chilled.

Cilantro Shrimp

Serves 4

YOU WILL NEED:

16 jumbo shrimp
1 garlic clove, minced
1 shallot, minced
2 lemons (cut 1 into 8 wedges, the other juiced)
$\frac{1}{4}$ c. dry white wine
1 bunch cilantro leaves, washed and roughly chopped
$\frac{1}{4}$ c. olive oil plus 4 tsp. (or cooking oil spray, olive oil flavored)
salt and pepper, to taste

Remove shells, wash and devein shrimp. Set aside.

In a medium bowl, combine the juice of one lemon, cilantro, shallot, garlic, $\frac{1}{4}$ c. olive oil, salt, and pepper, to taste. Set aside.

Heat 2 tsp. olive oil in a large skillet over medium-high heat. Arrange 8 shrimp and 4 four lemon wedges in the skillet and cook until shrimp turns an opaque pink, about 3–4 minutes per side. Remove ingredients from pan and set aside. Repeat process with remaining tsp. olive oil, second batch of lemon and shrimp and set aside.

Raise heat to high and pour wine into the skillet, scraping up any cooked bits of shrimp, and reducing wine by half. Pour bowl of lemon-cilantro marinade into skillet and heat, stirring constantly until shallots soften. Pour sauce over shrimp and lemon wedges and serve.

Shrimp Fajitas with Citrus Sauce
Serves 4–6

YOU WILL NEED:
1 1/2 lbs. shrimp, shells removed and deveined

FOR CITRUS SAUCE:
1 tsp. ground chipotle pepper, optional
1/4 c. fresh lime juice
2 tbsp. fresh cilantro leaves, finely chopped
1/4 c. fresh orange juice
1 tbsp. olive oil (or cooking oil spray, olive oil flavored)
4 garlic cloves, minced

Combine ingredients for Citrus Sauce.

Placed cleaned shrimp in bowl of citrus marinade and let sit about 20 minutes. Remove shrimp, discarding marinade, and grill or broil until shrimp are bright pink and opaque on both sides.

Serve with warmed flour tortillas and garnishes of guacamole, salsa, black bean dip, and fresh cilantro.

Cheese-Crusted Scallops

Serves 4

YOU WILL NEED:

$1/4$ c. soy parmesan cheese

1 shallot, minced

$1/2$ c. fresh bread crumbs

$1/4$ tsp. garlic salt

2 garlic cloves, minced

1 tbsp. olive oil (or cooking spray, olive oil flavored)

2 tbsp. fresh parsley, chopped

$1 1/2$ lbs. bay scallops

salt and pepper, to taste

Turn on broiler.

Place scallops in a small pot of boiling water and cook 2 minutes. Drain well and set aside.

In a skillet, heat oil over medium-high heat, and cook shallot and garlic until fragrant and soft. Place scallops and parsley in skillet and season to taste with salt and pepper. Gently stir to coat scallops and remove from heat.

Place scallop mixture in a baking pan and sprinkle with cheese and bread crumbs. Put under broiler until cheese is bubbly and golden brown.

Stir-Fry Scallops
Serves 2

YOU WILL NEED:

1 tbsp. canola oil

2 tsp. ginger, minced

1 c. asparagus spears, stems removed, lightly steamed

½ lb. sea scallops

2 plum tomatoes, sliced

¼ tsp. cumin

1 tsp. each rice wine vinegar, sesame oil, and soy sauce

In a large skillet or wok, heat canola oil.

Add scallops, tomatoes, ginger, and asparagus and cook, stirring constantly, until scallops become a flat white.

Add remaining ingredients and toss together until well coated.

Scallops in Watercress Sauce
Serves 4

YOU WILL NEED:

I lb. sea scallops

I bunch fresh flat leaf parsley

I bunch watercress

2 tsp. olive oil

2 shallots, chopped

I tsp. salt

Place: 1½ cups parsley, shallots, 1½ cup water, salt, and 1 cup watercress in a saucepan and bring to a boil. Reduce heat and simmer for about 30 minutes. Strain ingredients through a colander, reserving liquid and watercress mix.

Add oil to a large skillet over medium heat and season scallops on both sides with salt and pepper. Place the scallops in the skillet and cook five minutes, until golden brown. Turn scallops over and cook another 3 minutes. Repeat the process in batches, if necessary. Set aside.

Place reserved liquid in a saucepan and return to a boil. Place reserved watercress mixture and liquid in a blender and puree until smooth. Pour sauce over scallops before serving.

Shrimp "Fried" Rice
Serves 2

YOU WILL NEED:

I tbsp. canola oil

I zucchini, sliced like matchsticks

1/2 c. mixed vegetables of your choice: peas, carrots, broccoli florets

2 scallions, minced

2 1/2 c. cooked rice of your choice

1/2 c. small shrimp, peeled and deveined

2 tbsp. soy sauce

In a large skillet or wok, heat canola oil.

Add all ingredients, except soy sauce, and toss until shrimp are cooked through and pink. Add soy sauce and toss ingredients together until well coated.

Stir-Fry Chili Shrimp
Serves 2

YOU WILL NEED:

I tbsp. canola oil

3 1/2 lbs. shrimp, peeled and deveined

I tbsp. grated ginger

I garlic clove, minced

pinch of red pepper flakes

I tsp. each chili sauce, rice wine vinegar, apricot jam

In a large skillet or wok, heat canola oil. Add shrimp, ginger, pepper flakes, and ginger and toss until shrimp are cooked through and pink. Add remaining ingredients and toss well to coat.

poultry

Chinese Chicken and Black Beans
Serves 2

YOU WILL NEED:
1 tbsp. canola oil
2 c. broccoli florets
2 skinless, boneless chicken breasts, cubed
1 shallot, minced
$1/2$ c. canned black beans, drained
1 tbsp. soy sauce
1 tbsp. hoisin sauce
pinch of cayenne pepper

Heat canola oil in a wok or skillet over medium-high heat. Add chicken, broccoli, and shallot and stir often until chicken is cooked through. Add remaining ingredients and toss to coat thoroughly.

Roasted Lemon Chicken

Serves 6

YOU WILL NEED:

6 lemons

2 yellow onions, cut into quarters

10 garlic cloves, pressed

½ tsp. cayenne pepper, or more, to taste

1 tbsp. dried rosemary

3 split chicken breasts, skin removed

salt and pepper, to taste

Rinse chicken in cold water and pat dry. Preheat oven to 350 degrees. Rub chicken pieces with garlic and place garlic, chicken and onions in a coated roasting pan. Squeeze juice from lemons over chicken and then sprinkle on the rosemary, cayenne pepper, salt, and pepper, to taste.

Place in oven and roast for about 1½ hours, or until juices from chicken run clear. Serve with lemony juices poured over chicken and any vegetables you may serve.

Sweet and Spicy Chicken
Serves 4

YOU WILL NEED:
1 tbsp. olive oil
3 ripe, firm peaches, pitted and cut into quarters
6 garlic cloves
3 onions, chopped
1 lemon, cut into quarters
2 whole chicken breasts, skinless and boneless
$\frac{1}{2}$ tsp. ground chipotle pepper, or to taste
salt and pepper, to taste

Rinse chicken in cold water and pat dry. Preheat oven to 450 degrees.

Season chicken with salt and pepper, to taste, and place in a roasting pan. Sprinkle olive oil over chicken pieces and roast, uncovered, for 20 minutes.

Remove from oven and add remaining ingredients over and around chicken. Lower oven temperature to 375 degrees. Cover roasting pan and replace in oven for another half hour. Remove pan cover and roast for another 30–40 minutes, basting periodically.

Boy-O-Boy BBQ Chicken[20]
Serves 4

YOU WILL NEED:

1 2–3 lb. chicken, quartered and skinned

1 tbsp. olive oil

1 medium onion, chopped

2 cloves garlic, minced

1 tbsp. Dijon mustard

2 tbsp. maple sugar

$1/4$ c. fresh squeezed lemon juice

$1/2$ c. rice vinegar

$1/4$ c. soy margarine

$1 1/2$ c. ketchup

Wash and pat dry chicken pieces. Place chicken in a baking pan with dollops of soy margarine and bake for 30 minutes. In a skillet, heat the oil and add onion stirring until softened, about five minutes. Add garlic and stir until just colored. Be careful not to let the garlic burn. Add remaining ingredients and lower heat. Continue to stir and simmer, about 7 minutes. Remove from heat. Remove baking pan with chicken from the oven and apply sauce. Return to oven and bake for an additional 30 minutes, until juices run clear and sauce is nicely browned.

[20]LIQUID SMOKE adds a spicy, barbecue flavor to foods; used sparingly, a small bottle will last a very long time. Available in the spice section of your grocery store or specialty market.

Citrus Glazed "Fried" Chicken with Vegetables
Serves 4

YOU WILL NEED:

3 boneless, skinless chicken breasts, cubed

$1/3$ c. orange juice

2 tbsp. canola oil

$3/4$ c. water

$1/4$ tsp. ginger

1 tbsp. brown sugar

$1/2$ tsp. white pepper

2 tbsp. cornstarch

1 tbsp. paprika

1 c. onion, chopped

$1/2$ c. carrots, sliced into small pieces

$1/2$ c. mushrooms, lightly browned and drained

Rinse chicken in cold water and pat dry. Preheat oven to 350 degrees.

In a resealable baggie, shake together pepper, paprika, and cornstarch. Add chicken pieces and shake until coated evenly. Remove pieces from baggie and shake off excess. Reserve contents of baggie.

In a large skillet, heat oil over high heat. Place chicken pieces in skillet, turning occasionally to brown evenly. Remove chicken and place in a large baking dish. Add vegetables to baking dish. Set aside.

Carefully add baggie ingredients to used skillet and stir over medium heat until mixture is bubbling and well incorporated. Pour this sauce over chicken and vegetables and bake uncovered about 75 minutes, or until chicken juices run clear.

❖

Curry Chicken
Serves 2

YOU WILL NEED:

1 tbsp. canola oil
1 onion, thinly sliced
1 skinless and boneless chicken breast, cubed
1 garlic clove, minced
1 tsp. curry powder
pinch of cayenne pepper
1 tsp. Thai fish sauce
1/3 c. soy sour cream

Heat canola oil in a wok or skillet, over medium high heat. Add onion, chicken, garlic, and curry powder; stir often until chicken cooks through, about 5–7 minutes. Add remaining ingredients and toss to coat.

Herb-Crusted Chicken
Serves 4

YOU WILL NEED:

1 tsp. ground sage
1 dried bay leaf, crushed
1 tsp. dried thyme, ground
1 tsp. dried basil, ground
1/4 tsp. white pepper
4 tsp. olive oil (or cooking oil spray, olive oil flavored)
4 chicken breasts, skin removed

In a bowl, combine herbs and toss until well blended. Preheat oven to 350 degrees. With a brush or spoon, coat each chicken breast with 1 tsp. olive oil. Sprinkle herbs generously over chicken pieces until well coated and bake 45 minutes to 1 hour, until juices run clear.

Dandy Drumsticks
Makes about 30 mini-legs

YOU WILL NEED:
2 lbs. chicken drumsticks, skins removed

3 lemons, squeezed of their juice

$\frac{1}{3}$ c. olive oil

1 tsp. paprika

$\frac{1}{2}$ tsp. cayenne pepper (optional)

1 tbsp. dried rosemary

10 sprigs fresh thyme leaves

10 cloves of garlic, pressed

1 bunch flat-leaf parsley

salt and pepper, to taste

In a large bowl combine all ingredients and let marinate, refrigerated, for at least one hour. Heat a grill until very hot. Place drummettes on grill and cook for about 10 minutes, turning frequently so they cook evenly and turn a crispy, dark brown.

Fantastic "Fried" Chicken

Serves 4–6

YOU WILL NEED:

1 3–4 lb. chicken, cut into pieces
2 c. Italian flavored bread crumbs
2 eggs, beaten
salt and pepper, to taste
additional fresh herbs of your choice, including oregano, thyme,
tarragon, and/or chives
non-fat cooking spray

Preheat oven to 400 degrees. Wash and pat dry chicken pieces. Place bread crumbs, salt, and pepper and any additional herbs in a resealable quart-sized plastic baggie. Dip chicken pieces, about two at a time, into the egg and then place them in the plastic baggie. Seal baggie and shake until pieces are well coated. Shake off excess. Place chicken in a baking pan that has been coated with a non-fat cooking spray. Repeat until all pieces are coated. Bake in oven, rotating chicken pieces every 15 minutes until juices run clear, about 1 hour.

meat

Italian-Style Sausage and Peppers
Serves 6

YOU WILL NEED:
12 turkey sausages, sweet or hot (whichever you prefer)
4 peppers, choose a variety (red, yellow, green), thinly sliced
¼ c. olive oil
2 large yellow or sweet onions, thinly sliced

Heat oil over medium heat in a large skillet. Add onions and peppers and stir often until they caramelize, becoming brown, fragrant, and very soft, about 30 minutes. Remove onions and peppers and set aside.

In the same skillet or on a grill, cook sausages until evenly browned. Slice sausages lengthwise and top with generous portions of onions and peppers.

pasta

Linguine with Clam Sauce
Serves 4

YOU WILL NEED:
1 lb. linguine
2 dozen medium clams, scrubbed clean, soaked, rinsed, and drained
$1/4$ c. white wine
1 tsp. garlic, chopped
2 tbsp. fresh flat leaf parsley, chopped
1 tbsp. shallots, chopped
$1/2$ c. olive oil
2 tbsp. soy parmesan cheese
$1/4$ tsp. red pepper flakes
1 tbsp. soy margarine
salt and pepper, to taste

In a large skillet over medium-high heat, sauté shallots in olive oil until soft and translucent. Add garlic and stir, being careful not to burn. Add pepper flakes and parsley and stir, about 1 minute. Add wine and stir, until reduced by half.

To remove clams from their shells: After soaking, scrubbing, and draining clean, place clams in a pot of water, enough to just cover them. Cover pot, bring to a boil and lower heat. Let clams simmer about 2–4 minutes. Uncover and check to see if shells have opened. Drain, allow clams to cool before removing them from shells.

Chop in smaller pieces. Add clams to skillet, stir to coat and remove from heat. Add margarine and cheese and blend well. Add salt and pepper, to taste.

Prepare linguine according to package directions, drain and toss into clam sauce, coating pasta thoroughly.

Bow-Ties with Beans

Serves 6–8

YOU WILL NEED:

1 15-oz. can white beans, rinsed and drained

1 lb. bow-tie pasta (farfalle)

1 small red onion, diced

2 garlic cloves

⅓ c. fresh dill, chopped

⅓ c. fresh flat leaf parsley, chopped

½ c. soy parmesan cheese

¼ c. red wine vinegar

6 tbsp. olive oil

¼ c. fresh lemon juice

2 tbsp. soy sour cream

2 tbsp. Dijon mustard

Cook pasta according to package directions. Drain and set aside. In a blender or food processor add garlic, vinegar, lemon juice, and mustard and blend until well mixed. Slowly add in sour cream and olive oil and blend until sauce is well emulsified.

In a large serving bowl, pour blended sauce over pasta and toss well to coat. Pour beans, dill, onion, parsley, and capers over the top and toss to blend. Add fresh ground pepper, to taste and garnish with grated soy parmesan cheese.

Rice Noodles with Soy Sauce, Shrimp, and Scallions

Serves 4

YOU WILL NEED:

1 lb. shrimp, shells removed and deveined

2 12-oz. packages of rice noodles

1 bunch scallions, trimmed of white stems and sliced

3 tbsp. sweet black soy sauce

1 head of garlic, peeled of skins and mashed

2 tbsp. canola oil

6 tbsp. water, or as needed

6 tbsp. mushroom-flavored soy sauce

$\frac{1}{4}$–$\frac{1}{2}$ tsp. white pepper

$\frac{1}{2}$ c. plus 1 tbsp. brown sugar

Pour hot water over noodles in a strainer and use your hands to separate them, letting them soften. Set aside.

In a wok or skillet, heat oil over high heat. Add garlic and stir constantly until soft and fragrant. Place noodles and water in wok or skillet and stir about one minute before adding black soy sauce. Stir well and coat noodles. Add sugar, mushroom soy sauce, and pepper and stir until sugar melts and sauce thickens. Add scallions and shrimp and cook until shrimp becomes opaque and pink on both sides and scallions soften.

Marvelous Mac and Cheese
Serves 4

YOU WILL NEED:

1 1/2 c. grated soy cheddar cheese

8 oz. macaroni shells

3 tbsp. soy margarine

1 tsp. dry mustard

3 1/2 c. soy milk

3 tbsp. unbleached white flour

1/2 tsp. white pepper

1/2 tsp. dried oregano

1/2 tsp. dried basil

1 tsp. salt

3/4 c. bread crumbs

1/2 tsp. canola oil

Bring a large pot of water to a boil and follow package directions for cooking macaroni. Drain and set aside. Preheat oven to 350 degrees. In a large saucepan, melt margarine. Add flour and mustard and stir, about 3 minutes. Whisk in milk slowly without allowing sauce to come to a boil. Lift pan from heat to cool, if necessary. Continue to stir until sauce thickens. Remove from heat and add cheddar cheese, whisking until mixture is well blended. Season with salt and pepper, to taste and add macaroni, stirring mixture until shells are well coated. Pour mixture into a greased baking dish and set aside. In a separate bowl, blend herbs, oil, and bread crumbs. Sprinkle mixture over macaroni and cheese and bake in oven for about 20 minutes, until bread crumbs are browned and crispy.

Very Veggie Pasta
Serves 4

YOU WILL NEED:
1 lb. penne pasta
2 tbsp. olive oil
1 ½ c. vegetable broth
½ c. carrot, peeled and diced
1 c. broccoli florets
½ c. peas
1 c. soy parmesan cheese
2 sprigs of fresh thyme
1 bunch of fresh oregano, chopped

Bring a large pot of water to boil and follow package directions for cooking pasta. Bring 1 cup of broth to a boil in a medium skillet and season with thyme, oregano, and salt. Add broccoli and carrots and cook about 7 minutes. Add peas and cook until all vegetables are tender, about 3 minutes. Stir in olive oil and remaining stock. Drain pasta and toss into vegetable sauce. Garnish with soy parmesan cheese.

Cheesy Fettuccine
Serves 4

YOU WILL NEED:
I lb. fettuccine
I c. soy parmesan cheese
½ c. soy cream
4 tbsp. soy margarine

I bunch fresh spinach, rinsed well, drained, and roughly chopped
salt and pepper, to taste

Bring a pot of water to a boil and follow package instructions for cooking pasta. Melt 2 tablespoons margarine in a skillet over medium heat. Place spinach into the skillet and season with salt and pepper, to taste, cover. Lower heat and stir occasionally, until spinach softens. Remove lid and add ½ cup of soy cream; let cook another 4–5 minutes. Drain pasta and toss with remaining margarine and ½ cup parmesan. Add spinach sauce and serve with remaining parmesan, for garnish.

vegetarian-soy

Stuffed Eggplant
Serves 6

YOU WILL NEED:
3/4 c. couscous
4 small eggplants
I onion, peeled and diced
1/4 c. soy ricotta cheese
I yellow pepper, cored, seeded, and diced
I tbsp. lemon zest, chopped
1/4 c. fresh flat leaf parsley, chopped
1/2 lb. yellow and red cherry tomatoes, quartered
I tsp. salt
1/2 tsp. fresh ground pepper
2–3 tbsp. olive oil
1/2 head garlic, roasted[21]

Slice 3 eggplants in half lengthwise and score to remove strips of flesh from skins. Dice these strips and set aside. Save the eggplant shells.

Heat 2 tbsp. of olive oil in a large skillet over medium heat. Sauté onion until brown and tender, about 5 minutes. Add peppers, eggplant cubes, 1/2 tsp. salt, and 1/4 tsp. pepper. Cover pan and stir occasionally, about 6 minutes. Add extra olive oil if mixture gets too dry. Remove from heat and set aside.

In a heat-proof bowl, pour 1 c. boiling water over couscous. Cover and let sit about 15 minutes. Remove cover and fluff with a fork. Mix in zest, parsley, remaining salt, pepper, and ricotta cheese. Combine with remaining eggplant mixture, garlic and tomatoes. Stir to combine well.

Fill each eggplant shell with couscous mixture and bake covered in foil for 25 minutes. Remove foil cover and bake another 20 minutes until stuffing is crusty and browned. Sprinkle with parsley before serving.

---

[21]To roast garlic: wrap in foil and cook about 30 minutes in a 400 degree oven. Allow to cool before squeezing cloves from skins.

Greek Stuffed Grape Leaves
Serves 6

YOU WILL NEED:
24 grape leaves, rinsed and patted dry

FOR STUFFING:
$2\frac{1}{4}$ c. water
1 celery stalk, minced
$\frac{1}{2}$ c. toasted pine nuts or sunflower seeds
2 tbsp. olive oil (or cooking oil spray, olive oil flavored)
5 garlic cloves, minced
2 tbsp. fresh lemon juice
$1\frac{1}{2}$ c. onion, minced
$\frac{1}{2}$ tsp. salt
$\frac{1}{4}$ c. fresh parsley, chopped
1 tbsp. fresh mint, chopped
$1\frac{1}{2}$ c. brown rice, uncooked
salt and pepper, to taste

In a saucepan, bring rice and water to a boil. Cover and reduce heat. Simmer for about 45 minutes, until rice is cooked.

In a skillet, heat olive oil. Add salt, celery, and onion; sauté until soft. Add seeds or toasted nuts, garlic, salt, and pepper, to taste. Sauté for another 5 minutes. Add rice. Mix in mint, lemon juice, and parsley. Combine well.

To stuff grape leaves: Place a heaping teaspoon of stuffing at one end of leaf. Carefully and slowly roll grape leaf forward, folding sides inward halfway through rolling so that stuffing will not seep out.

When leaves are stuffed, lightly coat a baking pan with cooking oil spray or olive oil and bake stuffed leaves for 20 minutes at 350 degrees. Garnish with Lemon Sauce; recipe follows.

FOR LEMON SAUCE:

1 tbsp. fresh lemon juice

$1/2$ tsp. salt

1 box firm silken tofu

salt and pepper, to taste

In a blender or food processor, combine all ingredients until smooth. Drizzle over stuffed grape leaves and serve warm, at room temperature, or cold.

Stuffed Onions
Serves 8

YOU WILL NEED:

8 yellow medium onions, with peels

3 Yukon gold potatoes, peeled and cubed

1 c. fresh flat leaf parlsey

1 head of garlic, roasted[22]

1 c. fresh basil

10 oz. assorted mushrooms, sliced into strips

$1/4$ c. dry white wine

$2^1/2$ tsp. salt

$1/4$ tsp. fresh ground black pepper

olive oil cooking spray

Slice off top quarter of onions then wrap rest in foil before baking them $1^1/2$ hours at 450 degrees. Let cool before removing skins, and scoop out all but two layers, leaving a shell. Place shells in a baking dish and set aside. With remaining flesh, measure 3 cups and place in a food processor. Add parsley, basil, garlic flesh, $1^1/2$ tsp. salt, and $1/8$ tsp. pepper to onion flesh and puree until smooth.

Fill a large saucepan with water and bring to a boil. Add potatoes and boil until fork tender. Drain. Strain potatoes through a ricer and combine with onion mixture. Set aside.

Coat a skillet with cooking oil spray, add mushrooms, season with remaining salt and pepper, and cook until browned. Set aside.

Fill onion shells with layers of onion/potato mixture and sautéed mushrooms until full. Spray tops of stuffed onions with cooking oil spray. Pour wine into baking dish before baking about 30 minutes, or until onions are soft, golden and aromatic.

---

[22]See footnote 21 on page 128.

Stir-Fried Tofu
Serves 2

YOU WILL NEED:

1 tbsp. canola oil

1 tbsp. minced garlic

1 tbsp. minced ginger

2 c. mixed vegetables of your choice (minced carrots,
snow peas, sliced mushrooms)

½ lb. firm tofu, sliced into cubes

2 tbsp. soy sauce

2 tsp. rice wine vinegar

In a large wok or skillet, heat canola oil over medium high heat. Add vegetables, tofu, garlic, and ginger and toss until vegetables begin to soften. Add remaining ingredients and toss to coat thoroughly.

Mushroom Stir-Fry
Serves 2

YOU WILL NEED:

1 lb. mixed mushrooms: oyster, shiitake, button; sliced

3 scallions, minced

2 bunches bok choy, sliced and steamed until tender

1 tbsp. hoisin sauce

1 tbsp. soy sauce

In a large wok or skillet, heat canola oil over medium high heat. Add mushrooms, scallions, and bok choy and toss to cook until mushrooms begin to soften. Add remaining ingredients and toss to coat thoroughly.

Tofu with Tangy Onion Marinade
Serves 4

YOU WILL NEED:

I lb. block extra firm tofu, refrigerated until ready to serve

2 tbsp. soy sauce

2 tbsp. rice wine vinegar

I lime, juiced

2 tbsp. sesame oil

3 tbsp. extra virgin olive oil

I bunch fresh parsley, chopped

I bunch fresh cilantro, chopped

6 scallions, minced, discard most of white end

salt and pepper, to taste

In a mixing bowl, combine cilantro, scallions, and parsley. Add 1 tablespoon soy sauce, lime juice, olive oil, rice wine vinegar, and sesame oil. Stir mixture together well until herbs are coated. Let marinade sit for about ½ hour. Add salt and pepper, to taste.

Slice tofu into even cubes and drizzle marinade over the tops. Garnish with dollops of chili-garlic paste.

❖

▪ sweet treats ▪

Puddings

Banana-Nut Pudding

Serves 3

YOU WILL NEED:

1 ripe banana, cubed

1/4 tsp. cinnamon

1/4 c. brown sugar

1/4 tsp. nutmeg

1/8 c. pecans, toasted and roughly ground

1/2 c. uncooked rose rice

2 c. vanilla flavored soy milk

Soak rice in cool water for 30 minutes, to remove starch. Rinse and drain well. Add rice, and all other ingredients, except nuts and bananas, to a pot and stir to mix well. Leave pot uncovered and over medium heat bring to a simmer, stirring occasionally until rice falls apart, about 30 minutes. If rice pudding is too thick for your taste, add additional soy milk until you reach a suitable consistency. Remove from heat and allow pudding to cool before gently stirring in nuts and bananas.

❖

Powerful Pudding[23]

Serves 4

YOU WILL NEED:

2 c. soy or non-fat milk (lactose free, if necessary)
I tsp. vanilla extract
1/3 c. maple sugar or Sucanat
I 1/2 tbsp. arrowroot
I c. carob chips

Combine the maple sugar or Sucanat and arrowroot in a medium saucepan over medium heat. Add the milk and carob chips and heat, stirring constantly until mixture becomes thick, about 5–6 minutes. Remove from heat and stir in the vanilla. Let cool, stirring on occasion, so that the mixture will not stick to the pot. Place portions into serving dishes and refrigerate for up to an hour before serving.

---

[23]CAROB. You may have come across this name many times, but never tried it. Now is your opportunity! Carob is a wonderful sweetener. Not as rich as chocolate, carob is a wonderfully light substitute. Try carob chips in muffins, pancakes, and cookies.

Chocolate Pudding
Serves 6

YOU WILL NEED:
1 tbsp. vanilla extract

3 egg whites

1/2 c. cocoa powder

6 tbsp. cornstarch

3 c. vanilla flavored soy milk

6 tbsp. corn syrup

1/2 tsp. almond extract, optional

5 tbsp. granulated sugar or Sucanat

pinch of salt

Beat the egg whites in a large bowl until thick and frothy.

In a double boiler over medium heat, whisk together sugar, cocoa powder, cornstarch, and salt. Slowly add in corn syrup and milk and stir constantly so that ingredients do not stick to edges of the pot. Raise heat to high and whisk rapidly until ingredients come to a boil. Whisk one minute more before removing from heat.

Gently add several heaping spoonfuls of chocolate mixture to eggs and fold repeatedly to blend. Return this mixture to the double boiler over medium heat and stir constantly until pudding thickens. Remove from heat once again and add vanilla (and almond if desired) extract at this time. Place heaping dollops of pudding into serving dishes and refrigerate until chilled.

❖

Vanilla Pudding
Serves 6

YOU WILL NEED:
3 egg whites
3 c. vanilla flavored soy milk
6 tbsp. corn syrup
6 tbsp. granulated sugar or Sucanat
6 tbsp. cornstarch
pinch of salt
$^1/_2$ of a large vanilla bean, fresh

Slit open the vanilla bean and add the seeds and pod to a saucepan over medium heat. Pour in the milk and bring to a boil, whisking constantly. Remove milk and vanilla seeds (throw away pod) from heat and let cool to room temperature.

In a bowl, whisk egg whites until they become thick and frothy. Set aside.

In a double boiler over medium heat, whisk salt, cornstarch, and sugar. Slowly add vanilla-milk mixture. Bring water to a boil and whisk rapidly until ingredients blend and come to a boil. Whisk for another minute before removing from heat.

Gently add several heaping spoonfuls of vanilla mixture to eggs and fold repeatedly to blend. Return this mixture to the double boiler, over medium heat and stir constantly until pudding thickens. Remove from heat and distribute into serving dishes before refrigerating to chill.

cookies and brownies

Better-Than-The-Best Brownies
Yields about 1 dozen

YOU WILL NEED:

1 ½ c. unbleached white flour

5 eggs or 10 egg whites, beaten

1 tbsp. vanilla extract

2 c. Sucanat

½ tsp salt

¾ c. soy margarine, plus a dollop to grease the pan

½ c. unsweetened, dairy-free chocolate chips

½ c. grain-sweetened chocolate chips

Preheat oven to 350 degrees. Melt the margarine and chips over low heat in a large saucepan. Remove from heat and add vanilla and Sucanat. Beat in the eggs one at a time to make sure they are well blended. Grease a 9-x-13-inch baking pan. In a separate bowl, combine salt and flour well. Add chocolate mix and blend until smooth. Pour mixture evenly into greased baking pan and bake for 30 minutes. Allow to cool before slicing.

Coconut Oat Cookies
Yields 4 dozen

YOU WILL NEED:

1 c. shredded coconut

1 tbsp. vanilla extract

2 large eggs or 4 egg whites, room temperature

2$\frac{1}{2}$ c. rolled oats

1$\frac{3}{4}$ c. unbleached flour

1 tsp. baking soda

$\frac{1}{2}$ tsp. salt

8 oz. soy margarine

$\frac{3}{4}$ c. Sucanat

$\frac{3}{4}$ c. maple sugar

1 tbsp. water

Preheat oven to 375 degrees. With an electric mixer, cream the Sucanat, maple sugar, and margarine in a large bowl. Add in the vanilla, water, and eggs and combine well. In a different bowl, combine baking soda, salt, oats, flour, and coconut. Blend both bowls' ingredients together thoroughly and place spoonfuls of cookie dough on a cookie sheet. Allow space between cookies to avoid sticking. Bake 12 minutes.

Chocolaty-Chip Cookies
Yields 4 dozen

YOU WILL NEED:
2 c. grain-sweetened chocolate chips

1 tsp. vanilla extract

2 c. unbleached flour

$^3/_4$ tsp. baking soda

1 c. Sucanat

2 large eggs or 4 egg whites

$^3/_4$ c. maple sugar

8 oz. soy margarine, room temperature, plus a dollop for greasing

1 tsp. salt

Preheat oven to 350 degrees. With an electric mixer, cream the sugar and margarine until it becomes a light consistency. Add in the vanilla and the eggs, being careful not to over beat. Stir in the dry ingredients and then the chips. Place spoonfuls of dough onto a greased cookie sheet. Allow space between cookies to avoid sticking. Bake 12 minutes.

Positively Peanutty Cookies
Yields 4 dozen

YOU WILL NEED:
½ c. creamy all-natural peanut butter

1½ c. unbleached flour

½ tsp. baking soda

½ c. soy margarine, plus a dollop for greasing

½ c. Sucanat

1 large egg or 2 egg whites

½ tsp. vanilla extract

½ c. maple sugar

Preheat oven to 375 degrees. In one small bowl combine baking soda and flour. With an electric mixer, beat the margarine until smooth, on a low setting. Add the peanut butter, maple sugar, and Sucanat and beat well until ingredients are blended. Add in vanilla and egg. Lower mixing speed and add in half of the flour/baking soda. Mix manually with a spoon until well blended.

Place spoonfuls of dough onto a greased cookie sheet. Allow space between cookies to avoid sticking. Bake 10 minutes.

frozen desserts

Melon Sorbet
Yields about 1½ Quarts

YOU WILL NEED:
1¼ c. plus 2 tbsp. simple syrup
⅓ c. fresh lime juice
1 very ripe cantaloupe, about 2 lbs., rind removed and seeded

Slice melon into cubes and puree in a food processor. Place puree in a saucepan and simmer over medium-high heat, stirring occasionally, until reduced by one quarter. Remove from heat and set aside to cool.

In a bowl, mix together melon, lime juice, and simple syrup until combined. Freeze in an ice cream maker according to instructions.

Tropical Sorbet
Serves 6

YOU WILL NEED:

4 large, very ripe mangoes, pitted and cubed

$\frac{1}{2}$ c. granulated sugar or Sucanat

I tbsp. fresh lime juice

2 c. water

2 egg whites

In a saucepan over medium heat dissolve sugar into water. Remove from heat when sugar is thoroughly dissolved and pour in a bowl. Refrigerate, to chill.

In a blender, combine sugar water with remaining ingredients and blend until smooth. Freeze in an ice cream maker according to instructions.

Apricot Sorbet
Serves 6

YOU WILL NEED:

$\frac{1}{2}$ c. granulated sugar or Sucanat

$\frac{1}{2}$ c. fresh squeezed orange juice

I lb. fresh, ripe apricots, washed and halved to remove pits.

In a food processor add all ingredients and blend until liquefied. Place mixture in an ice cream maker and freeze according to instructions.

Fig Ice Cream
Serves 6

YOU WILL NEED:
⅔ c. granulated sugar or Sucanat
⅔ c. soy milk
⅔ c. water
1 lb. fresh, ripe figs, peeled

Place figs and sugar in a food processor or blender and blend until creamy. Add water and milk and blend until well combined. Place mixture in an ice cream maker and freeze according to instructions.

Citrus Sorbet
Serves 6

YOU WILL NEED:
4 large lemons, juiced and zest reserved
2 egg whites
2 c. water
2 c. granulated sugar or Sucanat

In a saucepan over medium heat dissolve sugar into water. Remove from heat when sugar is thoroughly dissolved and pour in a bowl. Refrigerate, to chill.

In a blender, combine sugar water with remaining ingredients and blend until smooth. Freeze in an ice cream maker according to instructions.

Peach Ice Cream
Serves 6–8

YOU WILL NEED:

2 c. fresh, ripe peaches, pitted, peeled and cubed
1 c. granulated sugar or Sucanat
2 tbsp. fresh lemon juice
1 egg white
½ c. water, plus 1 tbsp.

In a saucepan over medium heat dissolve sugar into water. Remove from heat when sugar is thoroughly dissolved and pour in a bowl. Let sugar water cool to room temperature.

In a blender or food processor, add sugar water and remaining ingredients and blend until smooth. Freeze in an ice cream maker according to instructions.

Blueberry Popsicles
Yield 12

YOU WILL NEED:
5 oz. fresh or frozen blueberries
32 oz. non-fat soy yogurt, vanilla flavored
3 tbsp. fresh squeezed lemon juice

Place 28 oz. of yogurt and 2 tbsp. juice in a blender and blend until combined. Transfer to a bowl and rinse out blender jar. Set yogurt/juice mix aside.

To blender add remaining juice, 4 oz. yogurt, and ½ c. berries and blend. You should have one cup of yogurt mix. Set aside.

Take popsicle molds and fill to the top, alternating between reserved yogurt blends. Swirl with a knife and freeze 25 minutes. Remove from freezer to insert popsicle sticks and return to freezer, at least 8 hours.

❖

pies

Graham Cracker Crust
Makes One 9-inch crust

YOU WILL NEED:
1 tbsp. canola oil
8 graham crackers, ground

Preheat oven to 325 degrees. Mix oil and ground graham crackers well and set aside. Lightly spray a 9-inch pie pan with cooking oil spray and press crust ingredients into pie pan, covering entire surface and pressing with even firmness. Bake 5 minutes and let cool.

Summer Berry Pie
Makes One 9-inch Pie

YOU WILL NEED:
1 baked graham cracker crust (pg. 146)
1 c. fresh strawberries, quartered
6 oz. silken tofu, firm
12 oz. silken tofu, extra firm
2 tbsp. maple syrup
1/4 tsp. vanilla extract
2 tbsp. granulated sugar or Sucanat

In a large bowl, pour sugar over strawberries and let sit at room temperature until juice forms, 5–10 minutes.

In a food processor add syrup, vanilla, and all tofu until well whipped. Add strawberry-sugar and blend until smooth, thick, and creamy. Carefully spread strawberry filling into pie crust and refrigerated until chilled and set. Garnish slices with fresh berries of your choice.

Squash Spice Pie
Makes One Pie

YOU WILL NEED:

1 baked graham cracker crust (pg. 146)

2 c. canned pumpkin flesh

2 12.3-oz. packages of firm tofu, light

(you will need 1 whole package plus 1/2 of the second package)

1/3 c. brown sugar

2 tsp. cinnamon

1/3 c. honey

1/2 tsp. nutmeg

1 tsp. ground ginger

1/4 tsp. cloves

1/4 salt

Preheat oven to 350 degrees. In a blender or food processor, puree all ingredients until smooth. Carefully spread squash filling into pie crust and bake one hour. Remove from oven and let cool before serving. The moist center of the pie will set when cool.

cooked fruits

Grilled Fruit

YOU WILL NEED:

USE ANY OR ALL OF THESE FRESH FRUITS

peaches, halved and pitted, $\frac{1}{2}$ tsp. sugar
or Sucanat sprinkled into peach centers
pineapples, skin discarded and sliced into $\frac{1}{2}$ inch slices,
sprinkle one side of each slice with sugar or Sucanat
pears, halved, seeded, and scored,
sprinkle incisions with sugar or Sucanat
bananas, leave skin on and slice, lengthwise, without
splitting in half, sprinkle incision with sugar or Sucanat
apples, peeled, halved, seeded, and scored,
sprinkle incisions with sugar or Sucanat
figs

Once fruits are prepared, grill the fruit skin side down on one end of narrow mesh double gridiron, with a hinge on one side. After sugar has melted and skins are charred, turn gridiron, fruit flesh down. Cook another 3–4 minutes. Note: apples and pears take longer to cook through, so if cooking with other fruits, start these 5 minutes earlier.

❖

Fruit Compote
Serves 4

YOU WILL NEED:

2 fresh figs, sliced

2 c. blackberries

4 apples (a sweet variety), peeled, cored, and sliced into quarters

I lemon, juiced, whole rind removed and reserved

1 1/4 c. water

4 tbsp. elderflower cordial

1/4 c. superfine sugar

2/3 c. soy yogurt

2 tbsp. honey

Place lemon zest, juice, elderflower cordial, sugar, and water in a large saucepan and simmer on medium heat for about 10 minutes. Add apples and simmer another 5 minutes, until tender. Remove from heat and place into a bowl. Add figs and berries to apple mixture and stir gently to combine. Cover and refrigerate until chilled. Serve on a plate with a heaping dollop of yogurt on the side. Drizzle yogurt and fruit with honey before serving.

Applesauce
Serves 4

YOU WILL NEED:
6 Macintosh apples, peeled and seeded
cinnamon, to taste
$^1/_2$ c. granulated sugar or Sucanat, or to taste

Bring a large pot of water to a boil and add apples. Cook until fork tender and drain. Place apples in a food processor and blend until smooth (leave some lumps for a chunky sauce). Add Sucanat and cinnamon, to taste.

Sweet and Spicy Applesauce
Serves 4

YOU WILL NEED:
6 medium-sized apples (a sweet variety, or
a blend of: Empire, Cortland, Macoun)
$^1/_3$ c. Sucanat or maple sugar
$^1/_2$ tsp. ground cloves
$^1/_2$ tsp. ground cinnamon
$^1/_2$ c. water
2 tbsp. fresh squeezed lemon juice

Peel, core, and dice apples into bite-sized pieces. Place apples in a saucepan with lemon juice and remaining ingredients; bring to a boil, stirring occasionally. Reduce heat and simmer for 20–30 minutes, until mixture is very soft. Remove from heat and allow sauce to cool. Mash mixture when cool enough until desired texture is achieved. Serve at room temperature.

Apple Butter
Yield 2 Cups

YOU WILL NEED:
1 c. apple cider
20 apples (Empire and/or Golden Delicious),
peeled, cored, and quartered
2 tbsp. fresh squeezed lemon juice
pinch of ground cloves
1 c. sugar or Sucanat
1 large cinnamon stick
1 tsp. ground ginger
$\frac{1}{2}$ tsp. ground cardamom
$\frac{1}{4}$ tsp. ground mace
$\frac{1}{2}$ tsp. ground nutmeg

In a heavy, large saucepan over medium-high heat, place all ingredients and cook, stirring frequently, until apples become thick and saucy, about 1 hour.

Lower heat to medium and transfer to a smaller saucepan. Continue to stir and cook until apple butter darkens and thickens, about another $2\frac{1}{2}$ hours. Remove from heat and allow to cool before storing in a Tupperware container, refrigerated, for up to 6 months.

❖

traveling snacks

On-The-Go Snack Mix
Serves 8–10

YOU WILL NEED:
1 c. raisins, golden, black, or a mixture
$\frac{1}{2}$ lb. almonds
$\frac{1}{2}$ lb. carob chips (optional)
1 c. sunflower seeds
1 c. pumpkin seeds

Mix ingredients together well and serve.

❖

Great Granola Bars

YOU WILL NEED:
2 c. crispy rice cereal (preferably from a health food label)

¾ c. raisins

1 c. rolled oats

2 c. granola

¾ c. dried apricots

½ c. peanuts

½ c. sunflower seeds

½ c. dried cranberries

½ c. honey, plus 2 tbsp.

¾ c. natural peanut butter

2 eggs or 4 egg whites, beaten

Grease a 13-x-9-inch baking pan and preheat the oven to 325 degrees.

Over low heat, melt the peanut butter and honey in a small pan. Set aside to cool.

In a large bowl, combine granola, raisins, oats, cranberries, apricots, peanuts, and sunflower seeds. Stir in the cooled peanut butter and honey mixture and coat dry ingredients well. Slowly mix in the eggs. Add rice cereal and press mixture gently into the greased baking pan until you have an even, single layer. Bake for 20–30 minutes until just browned along the edges. Remove from heat and allow granola to cool before cutting into squares. Try cutting with cookie cutters for a variety of fun shapes!

Now, you have a better idea of how rich and scrumptious alternative eating can be. Think substitution, *not denial.* Take time to cook, taste, smell, and enjoy these familiar (and not so familiar) flavors. They are all good, satisfying, and easy, and there are no painful and embarrassing consequences. Think of what a relief it will be to sit down to three meals a day and never suffer from an attack of diarrhea, cramps, bloating, or constipation! Revel in your new-found freedom and eat!

· eight

Your Child and IBS

Kids and IBS? Who would have thought that even children could suffer from it? We tend to believe that children, being young, active, and carefree, are immune to those external stimulants that can affect health. How could a young child of five, six, seven or eight, face the same challenges adults face? Kids don't get sick from the foods they eat, right? Wrong! In addition to the food allergies many children suffer from (like shellfish, nuts, and fruits, for example), kids can also experience the same symptoms demonstrated by adult IBS sufferers (cramps, gas, abnormal bowel movements) and a wide range of other related ailments, such as headaches, backaches, acne, not to mention obesity, and high blood pressure. How many of you have heard a child complain of a "tummy ache," only to discover that the ache is from anxiety? Perhaps the anticipation of the first day of school or an overnight sleepover is the catalyst for "pain."

Take your child[24] to the pediatrician if you notice that his/her symptoms have not disappeared within a couple of days. Don't hesitate to call your child's doctor to make sure a checkup isn't necessary. Your child may be shy about speaking up; it is your responsibility to speak up for them. Call your child's doctor repeatedly if you don't get an immediate response. It's always best to err on the side of caution when dealing with a child's well-being.

With that said, let us acknowledge that we live in a world where the kinds of pressures we face as adults may be felt by our children as well. Children are constantly bombarded by images of chaos and frenzy from the television, video games, and movies. We live in a fast-paced environment and ask our children to keep up. We rush our kids in the morning with little more than sugar- and fat-filled food for breakfast. We shuffle them off to school bleary-eyed and high on sugar. If we pack a school lunch, it probably contains a sandwich of processed luncheon meat, a sweet treat, and juice, also laden with sugar. If the school provides lunch, it's generally unsuitable. Some schools serve potato chips as a vegetable in addition to the soda and candy bars available in cafeteria vending machines. Caffeine and sugar content alone are enough to make our children sick. Are we sure they are eating enough? It's doubtful, given how ravenous they are at the conclusion of a school day! After school, your child may come straight home. In this day and age, however, it's likely she races off to some after-school activity, like sports, dance, art, or music. By the time she arrives home, all of you are exhausted. The last thing you want to do is prepare a time-consuming meal. In the meantime, your impatient child is eating a round of "snacks," too hungry to wait.

---

[24]For many of you reading this, you may be raising a grandchild as your own, or at the very least, making a tremendous contribution to your grandchild's upbringing. For the purposes of this text, children will be referred to as your child, regardless of the generation gap.

By the time dinner is ready, she is not interested in the dinner you've so painstakingly prepared (there's always room for dessert though!). The day has ended and you are both exhausted; the next morning brings another bout of fatigue. "Just a few more minutes, please!" is not what you need to hear when you're already running late. It's a pretty safe bet that many of you have had that battle in the morning.

With that brief picture of a typical day, it is evident that your child may suffer from IBS. Don't blame yourself. It is enormously hard to make the very best choices for our children. Twenty-four hours just doesn't seem like enough time. We are all challenged to accomplish as much in a day as we can. Our children, unfortunately, fall victim to this pressure as well. Although the school environment frees adults up, children get little "time out." They face the same emotional and social challenges as grownups—making friends, maintaining good, happy relationships, and avoiding conflict. Children want to be liked by their peers as well as their superiors. They may attempt to assert their independence but they need your guidance and unconditional support. Children are expected to excel academically, athletically, and socially; falling short in any one area may be perceived, by a child, as failure. And your attempt to be supportive may be perceived as pressure.

Coupled with this is a poor diet. Young people are seduced by fat and sugar, fast food, and flashy packaging that promise super-duper sizes and more. We, as parents, are engaged in an uphill battle to limit their cravings for sweets and greasy foods. More often than not, we surrender to the desires of our children. Who wants to deal with screaming or crying in the supermarket or restaurant? Giving in is the path of least resistance. But our kids suffer the consequences of eating unhealthy foods that cause innumerable problems. We comfort their tummy aches with a warm hug and a lecture on the evils of junk food. In the end, everyone feels badly.

If children are living lifestyles that may promote the onset of IBS, we must commit to making the right choices for them. This may involve eliminating some extracurricular activities, changing eating habits, or having "quiet" time. Think about what your child does right before dinner. Is he spending time in front of the television, or playing with a sibling? Could you use help preparing the meal? And what *is* for dinner? Is it a high-fat, high-sodium, frozen meal, or is it takeout, again? You can't be too sure about what's in those meals! If you cook together, try something fun and healthy that the whole family will benefit from and enjoy.

We all know how stress can impact an adult's life. Stress can have a great impact on the lives of children, too. And they don't necessarily know what's bothering them. Food is the building block for a healthy, strong, energetic body. The body can only function at its peak if it is consistently fueled by healthy food. A wholesome diet will not only stimulate the body, but the mind. With good nutrition, a child is able to able to think more clearly and act calmly.

You may be saying to yourself, "Get my child to stop eating junk food? I don't think so." If your child is suffering from IBS or, if you feel that you would like to change your child's eating habits, you must take charge! Although this may sound like a tall order, when your child's health is at risk it is certainly worth the effort! Remember, you are the adult with the ability to differentiate between healthy and unhealthy. Take advantage of your power and let your child learn from you. Share your newly gained knowledge about proper nutrition with your child. It will amaze you to discover how receptive a child can be! You don't need to have all the answers right now. If your child has reached an age where she can explore vegetarianism, share in the process with her. Search together for vegetarian recipes that your family will enjoy.

It is much easier to change the dietary habits of younger children. They are more curious, more responsive and willing to please the adults around them. Making better food choices now lays a blueprint for the remainder of their lives. They will always return to their more familiar, healthy ways if they have this blueprint to work with. A deviation from proper eating will be temporary. Your child will always return to healthy foods if you encourage good eating habits from birth.

Finally, some helpful tips:

❖ Begin the adaptations slowly if this feels more reasonable for you and your child. If you know that three-day-a-week meal preparation is too difficult, don't try to alter your food choices for these nights. The idea is to incorporate changes gradually, so good eating habits are developed over time.

❖ Begin to buy fewer high-sugar, high-fat foods at the grocery store. Stay away from the chips, cakes, doughnuts, and ice cream. Try to find alternatives to these items in your health food store. Better still, shop for fruits or pretzels (but beware of the sodium content). Bake a healthier cake together; you'll both enjoy the process.

❖ Learn about new food together. Plan a "special trip" to the health food or grocery store and "hunt" for a list of foods, like tofu, tempeh, tamari soy, and flaxseed oil. If you decide to embark on this adventure, do so after you've both eaten. Food shopping on an empty stomach is an invitation to revert to old habits.

❖ Get your child cooking! Sure, it's not easy. It takes time and patience. But give it a try! Cook with your child on a weekend when you're both not rushing to get ready for the following school/work day. A rainy day is perfect for a "joint" cooking venture.

❖ Plan ahead! Think about foods to include in your child's lunchbox. If the school provides lunch have your child choose a new healthy snack to eat later in the day. Place it in a decorated bag for him to take to school. Let your child select a favorite cereal at the health food store. Ask him for a dinner suggestion. It may surprise you to see how daring he is in making a selection. Encourage your child to choose "safe" alternative foods when dining out.

❖ Speak to other parents and caretakers who may be responsible for your child. Let them know that your child may have food allergies. Don't be afraid to send along food you know is appropriate. Your effort will be appreciated!

❖ Stay positive and persevere! If you say aloud to yourself, "I don't want to eat this" or, "This is too hard," your child will follow your lead. If you're negative about trying new foods, your child will be too. Be enthusiastic! If you hate a particular food, so be it. You won't have it again, but your child may enjoy it. You'll never know unless you make the attempt and serve as the role model.

❖ A recent clinical trial has shown that Enteric-coated peppermint oil capsules have significantly improved IBS symptoms in children ages 8–17, weighing over ninety-nine pounds (more extensive studies are necessary). Speak with your child's doctor about this treatment and any possible side effects.[25]

The younger the child, the easier it is to introduce and maintain proper eating. Certainly it's a good idea to do this whether your child suffers from IBS or not. But if your young one does have IBS symptoms, it is quite easy to alter their dietary intake without too much difficulty. Children, particularly little ones, are impressionable and will absorb the lessons and practices you teach them rapidly.

[25]Dr. Donald J. Brown, HerbalGram, *The Journal of the American Botanical Council and the Herb Research Foundation*, Austin, TX 2001, Number 52, 22–23.

If your child is a toddler, it is the perfect time for you to explore ways for good eating to become a natural and desirable goal for her. If you start now, there will be less to contend with later on. Take advantage of this impressionable age. Encourage her to try all different types of fruits, vegetables, soy products, and legumes. Steer clear of fast foods, high fat, and refined sugar. Allow your child's palate to be seduced by fruits, syrups, and baked vegetables containing natural sweetening agents.

Since your child will be hosting, as well as attending parties, dates, and school events, he will unavoidably be introduced to refined sugars and fast foods. Face it head on! Don't think your child won't try something that he hasn't tried before—that's what children do! And if it has pretty packaging in bright primary colors, he'll run toward it! Be honest with your children, but don't badger them with negative commentary. These goodies are tasty and when coupled with friends and fun they're just too hard to resist. You don't want your children making healthy dietary choices out of guilt. You want them to know what's best for them. It's okay to enjoy the "bad stuff" once in awhile. Children are observant and, if given the proper tools to make the right decisions, they will do so.

When children reach elementary school they are at a critical age in their development. They are now able to differentiate, with more clarity, between good food and bad. By age six, a child is able to comprehend that healthy food equals a healthy mind and body. Discuss with your child how the body functions much like a car that needs to fill its engine with proper fuel to run well. If your child loves sports or dance, she may appreciate this lesson even more. Use the analogy as often as you see fit. It helps your child appreciate that the positive choices she makes have a positive impact.

Let your children chart the foods they enjoy most and least. Encourage them to create their own shopping list of foods they would like to prepare and eat. Children want to be able to feel they are making a contribution. Give them the

chance to do so! Food is a wonderful tool for practicing independence and experimenting with something new. Encourage
your children to take advantage of all the wonderful varieties
of foods available to them.

Have your child prepare his own lunch (or snack) for
school. With your watchful eye he will love the opportunity
to consider his options. It may surprise you to witness how
much more he will eat if he has prepared everything himself.
He will be bursting with pride.

Pre-adolescence is a trying time. As they contend with
school and extracurricular activities younger adolescents are
also establishing closer bonds with their peers. They are
straddling the high, risky fence of independence. Children at
this age still rely on and need their loved ones for support
and guidance. At the same time, they are experimenting and
forming relationships with people who will influence their
decisions and opinions. To compound this, hormones are
beginning to spin their complex webs, and have a great
impact on the pre-adolescent's physical and emotional state.

Most importantly, many girls this age may begin to view
their bodies in a new and often disturbing way. Pre-adolescent girls may become self critical and self-conscious. You
cannot look the other way! A long pattern of self-damaging
behavior may be established that impacts both her emotional and physical wellness. Too much talk about dieting should
be acknowledged, discouraged, and dismissed immediately.
Be aware of your daughter's behavior and body image. And
do not be afraid to confront her, if what you see and hear
disturbs you. Open dialogue can make all the difference in
how your daughter feels about herself now, and who she
will become in the future.

If you've already established a dialogue with your child
about food by the time they are full-fledged teens, this is
great, and you need to continue! If you haven't, start now! If
you are just beginning to change your own eating habits, be
open and upfront with your child about why you are making

the change. Invite your child (and even his friends on occasion) to prepare a meal with you. This is a wonderful way to introduce new foods and expand his knowledge about nutrition. In addition, take advantage of this opportunity to discuss other topics of concern with your child; often, those social and emotional concerns are somehow easier to approach over food!

Enjoy the freedom that food allows you and your child to experience. Explore, experiment, and take as much time as you need to develop your child's interest in what she eats. It will make you happy and proud to know you've helped the people you cherish most!

· nine ·

Exercises for Sufferers

Yoga and Tai Chi are the best exercises for IBS sufferers. They help you not only physically, but mentally and emotionally as well. The movements in both these exercises gently strengthen the muscles of the entire body. The rhythmic breathing and gentle stretching movements increase flexibility of the muscles, as they massage the internal organs. The repetitive movements enable the body to slow down and function at a steady pace. This will help your circulation and digestion, as well as soothe your nervous system. After doing yoga or Tai Chi you will find a greater ability to relax and think more clearly. Your physical responses to certain external stimuli will be eased, and you will feel more in control.

This chapter will highlight some movements of yoga. Yoga can be practiced by anyone, regardless of age, sex, or physical capability. Read carefully and practice slowly. Although the exercises (or positions) are not difficult, you will want to be sure to take your time so you avoid straining. You will soon begin to see that you're feeling better, calmer, and thinking more clearly. Remember: Your mind and body work in tandem. You can't neglect one without feeling the effects on the other. Yoga and Tai Chi (as well as several other forms of movement) take advantage of this mind-body connection and work effectively on both.

Before You Begin

FIRST AND FOREMOST, check with your doctor before starting any movement or exercise program. You need to make certain that you are in satisfactory condition before proceeding. Now, it's time to get moving!

Before you begin, make sure you are wearing something comfortable (i.e., loose fitting or stretchy). You should be able to move without restriction. Find a room or outdoor space where you will not be disturbed and where you may exercise quietly. Yoga should be practiced in an environment conducive to calm, and free of outside distractions and noise.

Always begin your movements with five minutes of quiet, soothing meditation or relaxation. Now, you will start yogic breathing. This will clear your mind. As you practice the positions, remember your breathing, maintain a still face with soft eyes and take your time. Exercise slowly and do not force yourself. Over time, your flexibility will increase, as will the ease with which you move.

Yogic Breathing

THE MOST IMPORTANT aspect of yoga, or any exercise for that matter, is breathing. It sounds silly, because we take breathing for granted. It is something we do without thinking. Right? Although this is true, you may be surprised to learn how hard the proper breathing technique is when you're exercising. Before you know it, you're out of breath, feeling light headed and ready to quit. When you practice yoga, you must breathe at a steady and rhythmic pace in order to maintain quiet and focus as you move. This will enable your body to properly receive maximum physical and mental benefits. When you breathe properly, you take in the oxygen necessary to metabolize food successfully. This means that the vitamins and minerals ingested from the foods you eat can be absorbed into the bloodstream. In addition, proper breathing allows the body to rid itself of gaseous waste, particularly carbon dioxide. The entire process of metabolism requires oxygen to function the way it should. Interestingly, most of us breathe in a "shallow" manner. That is, when we take in air, we do not take in enough breath to fill our entire lungs with air. Generally, we use only the top part of our lungs to breathe, which actually leaves the rest of our lungs hungry for oxygen. This prevents the complete, successful elimination of waste.

In order to breathe properly for yoga, you must begin at the diaphragm and pull in air through the nose. Exhaling carbon dioxide should also take place through the nose. This taking in and pushing out of air should be done slowly, comfortably, and at a steady pace. You should feel your ribs expand and contract with every breath.

INHALATION	EXHALATION
Proper inhalation requires taking air in through the nostrils, where it passes down the trachea and into the lungs. When it reaches the diaphragm, the lungs should expand.	Proper exhalation requires the lungs to contract, propelled by the diaphragm, forcing noxious waste up out of the lungs, through the trachea and expelled through the nostrils.

In addition to the physical benefits of proper breathing, the mental benefits are significant. How many times have you been told during moments of agitation or stress to "take a deep breath." This is actually very sound advice. When you breathe in deeply, you give your brain the oxygen it needs to metabolize successfully. Deep breathing calms the brain and the rest of the body. This "calming" has a profoundly positive effect on mental clarity and emotional balance. With practice and in time proper breathing will allow you to deal with potentially volatile situations without stress. In addition, correct breathing can immediately (and for the long term) improve your emotional responses to difficult circumstances.

Beginning Exercises

IN ORDER TO practice yoga successfully and with ease, it is important for you to prepare your body for the positions required. You need to relax to breathe properly and move correctly. These five minutes will give you ample time to quiet your body and alleviate tension.

During this time your *mind* should also become tranquil. Try to focus on pushing away any thoughts you may have; any worries you have or any concerns about what you must do later in the day. Clear your mind, and your body will begin to rid itself of tension, discomfort, and anxiety. If you are chilly, lie under a blanket. Your body should not only be calm but also warm in order to work efficiently.

The Corpse Pose

Lie flat on your back, arms out to the side, feet a distance apart from one another. Keep your eyes closed and concentrate on your proper, yogic breathing. All extremities should be straight, but not tensed. Remain relaxed in this position for about five minutes or until you are ready to move on.

Neck Rolls

So much tension is held in the neck and shoulder region. These areas should be relaxed and loose before proceeding to other movements.

I. Allow the head to fall forward, resting the chin toward the chest. Feel the stretching in the back of the neck. Slowly, lift the head and gently let it fall backwards until you are looking straight up. You should gently stretch as though trying to touch the back of your head to your spine. Repeat several times, like an exaggerated "yes."

2. With your gaze forward, gently drop your right ear toward your right shoulder and hold it there for a moment. Raise your head up slowly and continue bending your neck until the left ear is reaching toward the left shoulder. Repeat several times.

3. With your gaze forward, turn your head slowly to the right, without turning your shoulders. Turn your head back to the front and repeat to the left. Repeat back and forth several times, like an exaggerated "no."

4. Begin with the head down toward the chin and rotate it gently all the way around, clockwise. Repeat several times before rotating counter-clockwise. Do not strain the neck and stop if there is any pain. Your muscles need to become relaxed and used to this movement, so don't push it! Your flexibility will increase in time, but **remember to breathe!**

The Sun Salutation

Yoga exercise often begins with The Sun Salutation. This series of movements serves as a wonderful warm-up. It can be practiced often before you move on in your routine. These twelve movements are particularly beneficial to beginners, the elderly, and people who may be particularly stiff or without much flexibility. Remember to breathe, and try to keep your mind clear and focused.

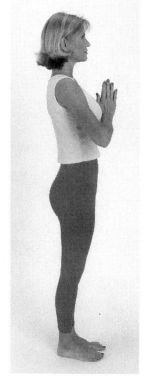

STARTING POSITION: Stand straight, face forward, eyes relaxed, with feet together and arms at your sides. Take a deep breath and begin.

I. Center the body by taking a breath and exhaling. As you exhale, lift the hands and place them in front of the chest, as if in prayer.

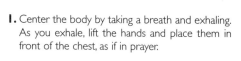

2. Keeping your legs straight, lift the arms up and back over your head with your hands still together. Follow the movement with your gaze, arching your back and pushing your hips forward. Inhale.

3. As you exhale, bend forward as far as you can, reaching your arms, hands, and head toward the floor. Keep your knees straight if you can.

4. With your hands on the floor, inhale and reach your right leg back keeping it straight while bending your left leg, until it reaches a 90-degree angle; you should be in a lunge position. Lift your gaze up and ahead and hold.

5. Bring your gaze down toward the floor and straighten your bent left leg back until it meets your right, with your hands on the floor, arms straightened. Your body should now be in the plank position, similar to a push-up.

6. As you exhale, drop your knees to the floor, lower your forehead and chest down to the floor as well. Keep the hips and the elbows bent up.

7. Inhaling, slowly bring your gaze up and arch the back. Keep elbows bent and shoulders relaxed as you point your toes, relaxing the hips on the floor, legs parallel to each other.

8. Exhale and push your hips up in the air, keeping your head facing down between your arms, hands on the floor. Try to straighten your knees and arms and breathe.

9. Now, inhale and bring your right leg forward in the same 90-degree bended lunge as before, keeping your left leg straightened behind you and your gaze toward the sky.

10. Keeping your hands on the floor, bring your left leg forward until your left foot meets your right and bend your head down toward your knees. Exhale and straighten your limbs if you can.

11. Inhale and slowly reach your arms up and back over your head, arching your hips forward as done in figure 2.

12. Exhale slowly and straighten your body, gazing forward, hands relaxed at your sides, feet together, back to beginning position. Inhale and exhale deeply before starting the Sun Salutation again. Repeat until the movements flow smoothly.

The Forward Bend

This series of movements massages the abdominal organs, including the GI tract. It helps to relieve constipation and stimulates proper functioning of the colon. Practice until each position flows into the next.

I. Sit on the floor with your legs straight in front of you, hips, shoulders, and neck relaxed, gazing ahead. Flex the feet gently and breathe.

2. As you inhale, stretch both arms up over your head, elbows by your ears, and think of lengthening the spine up to the sky.

3. Exhaling slowly, bend your body forward at the hips, lowering your arms and head toward your knees, keeping your legs as straight as possible. Hold this position for about ten seconds and come back to starting position. Repeat this movement three times, if you are comfortable.

The Cobra

The Cobra is wonderful for increasing the flexibility of the spine, massaging the organs of the GI tract and releasing pressure in the abdomen. Practice until each position flows easily together in one fluid motion.

1. Begin by lying facedown on the floor, head turned to the side, legs straight but relaxed, toes down on the floor and turned in toward each other. Arms should be bent at the elbows, hands by your head.

2. As you exhale, turn your head toward the floor, chin tucked in toward your chest, forehead resting on the floor. Place your hands close to your shoulders, fingers pointing ahead.

3. Slowly inhale and lift your head straight up and back, lifting your shoulders and chest toward the sky. Remember to breathe and hold the position for about ten seconds. Exhale slowly as you return to the starting position, and repeat three times, if you are comfortable.

The Spinal Twist

The Spinal Twist helps to relieve digestive problems, including constipation and bloating. It also helps to relieve problems related to the back and hips.

1. Begin by sitting on your heels, with your back straight, gaze forward, knees bent beneath you. Lean slightly over so that your weight is toward your left side.

2. Lift your right knee and place your right foot on the floor; keep your left foot tucked underneath you.

3. Lift your right foot so that it is on the outside of your left knee and slowly twist toward your right side. Keep your right arm straight, with your hand on the floor. Look toward your right and over your right shoulder. Keep your left hand on your right ankle. Hold this position and breathe for about ten seconds, keeping your buttocks on the floor and your chest lifted up. Release the position and repeat on the other side.

Modified Cat's Pose

This position almost instantly relieves pressure and bloating associated with gas.

1. Get down on all fours, fingers facing forward, toes either tucked under or pointed back, face to the floor, back straight.
2. Slowly, inhale and arch your back, lifting your gaze skyward and relaxing the abdominal area, so that the buttocks are lifting up, the stomach falling toward the floor. Return to starting position and repeat several times.

   If necessary, keep the elbows bent on the floor, chest down, while the buttocks reach toward the sky, like a cat stretching. This position has the same effect, but may be more comfortable for you.

Final Relaxation

Return to **The Corpse Pose** (page 169) for this position. Lie on your back, eyes closed, legs softened in front of you, arms relaxed out to your sides. Keep your neck and head relaxed and focus again on your  breath. Inhale and exhale slowly and deeply.

Starting with your feet, and moving to your legs, buttocks, shoulders, and head, think specifically of each area and focus on the complete relaxation of each, one by one. As you do this, you should begin to feel heavy in your body and light in your mind. Everything should become still and calm. Remain in this position, focusing on your breath, for at least 10 minutes. If you wish, play soft, soothing music, at a low volume. You may find that music helps you to focus and relax.

Practice any of these positions as often as possible. If time is an issue, practice your breathing whenever you find the time. On your way to work, when you wake in the morning, while watching television, or just before bed. Learning to breathe correctly is critical to the success of your exercise program. Make the attempt and you'll be proud of your accomplishment. The more you practice, the easier it will become and the more beneficial it will be to you.

· ten ·

Questions to Ask Your Doctor

This chapter has been included to assist you when you visit with your physician. It is meant to help you think about the things you need to know, as you explore the causes and ways of controlling your condition. And, because it can be difficult to discuss your battle with IBS (much less remember all the questions you may have about it) the list below will serve as a guideline. Oddly enough, we sometimes forget the questions we have when we are face to face with the very person who can give us with the right answers! Space is also provided for you to add any additional questions or comments you may have.

1. How can I be sure IBS is what I'm suffering from?
2. Should I be tested for other conditions and how should I prepare for the tests?
3. Can I be lactose intolerant?

4. Should I consider drug therapy? What are the possible side effects?
5. Should I take a fiber supplement?
6. Can you tell me more about alternative medicinal treatments?
7. Can you tell me about food allergies?
8. Might it be wise for me to seek psychological counseling?
9. Am I a candidate for antidepressant medication?
10. Is there anything I can do to alleviate and curtail my symptoms once they've been triggered?
11. Can you help me locate an IBS support group in my area?
12. _____
13. _____
14. _____
15. _____

No matter what, do not feel embarrassed about your condition. No one but you can take control of your body. Use your physician as a source of information and assistance. Be forthcoming about your symptoms and allow your doctor to share his/her knowledge with you. A visit with the doctor is a great source of comfort. Don't hesitate to solicit as much as you can from him or her.

· eleven ·

Helpful Hints and Final Suggestions:
Living Well With IBS

By now, you may be feeling overwhelmed by all the information and daunted by the notion of making significant lifestyle changes. This is perfectly understandable. The thought of living with an incurable (though possibly temporary) condition is not a pleasant one. And the effort it may take to feel better is challenging, at the least. Certainly, it takes hard work to improve the quality of your life, but think for a moment about all the things you already do in your daily life that have become second nature: brushing your teeth, combing your hair, doing your laundry, preparing a meal, and taking your vitamins. These are things we do every day that we don't even think about. Just as you've gotten into the habit of attending to these daily activities, you can learn to get in the habit of making adaptations. Whether it is trying new food from the market, or inquiring about the proper exercise classes offered at your local gym, you can become more conscientious about obtaining and maintaining good health!

It is important to know that if you are living with IBS, you should not feel pressured to make food choices that seem acceptable in social situations. Although you may not feel uncomfortable about exchanging dialogue about your condition, try to relax so your symptoms aren't aggravated and you have time to hear suggestions. Don't worry about the pressure to eat that tempting trigger food during a social occasion. Nobody but you will suffer if you indulge. Of course, these goodies are tempting and you may find them impossible to resist, but visualize the consequences you may face if you don't resist! If it is your diet that primarily triggers your symptoms, you must make significant alterations as soon as possible. You will see changes almost immediately and you'll feel like a new person. How liberating it will be for you to *not* have to worry about your physical symptoms day after day, and when you have no thought of bathrooms, flatulence, pain, bloating, and misery! Take a few minutes to organize the ways in which you may begin to make dietary alterations. Write the changes down, if that helps. Plan your meals the night before, if having a guide will enable you to make proper eating decisions. Remember to leave the house with appropriate snacks, if you won't have much time to eat. Plan ahead in order to insure a physically comfortable day.

Here are some quick **reference tips** for you to keep in mind:

1. **Learn about IBS and visit with a physician about your condition.**
2. **Become familiar with the factors that trigger your symptoms**: foods, external stress—refer to your logs.
3. **Travel with snacks!** Do not let yourself get too hungry before your next meal. This is a sure way to increase your chance for developing symptoms.

When you're dining out, take your time looking over the menu. Choose those foods you know are safe or inquire about options. There is no harm in asking if a meal can be served without a heavy cream sauce, or with egg whites only, for example. Although many restaurants may not be able to make non-dairy substitutions for you, they can certainly make omissions. Feel free to ask questions about the menu. Restaurant servers are there not only to deliver your food, but also to help you interpret the menu. Take advantage of their knowledge and be sure you are comfortable with the information they provide. Most restaurant staff are very accommodating. If they are not, don't be shy about leaving. Obviously, if you are seated with a group, this may not be an acceptable alternative. Let your server know, however, that you suffer from food allergies, and he should be more than willing to grant your special requests.

Make every effort to locate the bathroom as soon as you enter an eating establishment. This information is invaluable, since it may be necessary to "run" there immediately. Don't be shy about asking the "bathroom" question; it has been asked many times before and making the inquiry is far less embarrassing than making a bee-line for an unknown location. If you are having take-out, you can certainly make the same requests over the phone. But take some time to explore your neighborhood and find the names of those restaurants that offer a good selection of foods that will not trigger your symptoms.

4. **Read labels at the grocery/health food store before you decide to purchase items**. Prepare yourself before you stroll down the aisles of the grocery store. Silly as it sounds, we often race through the grocery store and pick up only those things we need and are familiar with. Study those items you may have

overlooked over the years. Try soy milk instead of or in addition to non-fat cow's milk. If you would rather not throw away egg yolks, pick up a container of egg substitute. Look through the international (or imported food) section of the grocery store and pick up a bottle of soy sauce or a spice you have never tried before; adapt your favorite recipes to suit them.

5. **Drink lots of water!**
6. **Reduce your intake of fats, alcohol, tobacco, and caffeine**.
7. **Be wary of the *kinds* of fibers you eat (soluble vs. insoluble).** Whenever possible, eat insoluble fibers *cooked*, not raw.
8. **Avoid buying that gas-inducing pack of gum!** If you are desperate for some kind of sweet have jellybeans, sugar-free hard candies, or mints (in moderation, of course). In addition, avoid chocolate or fatty snacks, like fried potato chips. Opt for baked varieties instead.
9. **Consider traditional behavioral therapies, as well as alternative treatments, such as psychological counseling, Yoga, and Tai Chi.** You may find that the external factors in your life have a greater impact on your symptoms than your diet does. If this is true, you will benefit from the meditative exercises offered in this book. Try to abandon your feeling of embarrassment. No one will laugh or make fun. These exercises support the individual's capacity to help him/herself. Further, don't worry about your physical shortcomings. Even those individuals who are physically challenged can take part in these forms of movement. Don't forget: these forms of movement are geared toward calming the mind—not rigorously moving the body. These exercises are addictive because of how they make you feel emotionally and mentally.
10. **Prepare foods using healthier methods.** Grill, roast, bake, or steam rather than frying. Use spices

and seasonings freely in your dishes. They add flavor without the fat that can act as a trigger. Omit frying from your cooking. Bake, stir-fry, oven-"fry," steam or grill instead. Choose lean cuts of meat, trim off any visible fat, and remove skin. Prepare eggs without the yolks; use egg substitutes (whites only). Increase your consumption of fish as you decrease your consumption of red meats. Choose vegan or soy substitutions for meat-based dishes. A good health food store will offer an array of substitutions for a variety of your favorites. Everything from "burger" patties to hot dogs and "chicken" nuggets are wonderfully tasty alternatives. Cook in bulk. Choose foods that you and your family eat often and, make lots of it. Rice, beans, and breads are popular items that freeze well and may be reheated in a pinch. In addition, prepare safe snack foods in quantities you may use every day over an extended period of time. If you do not have the opportunity to cook an appropriate meal the On-The-Go Snack Mix (pg. 153) or Edamame (pg. 86) in the Recipe chapter are quick and easy to prepare and make wonderful on-the-go treats that are perfectly safe.

11. **Seek out others who share your condition.** It is not only *helpful* to know you are not alone, but you will have others with whom to share resources and suggestions. Speak to your loved ones. Let them know about your condition and explain the reality of it. Help them to understand that it is imperative you alter your eating habits. Reassure them that they do not have to do the same, but they may want to join you in making the change anyway. Let them know that you are learning something new and that you would welcome their support and partnership in this new venture. Your family will appreciate your honesty and enthusiasm to share.

POTENTIALLY HARMFUL FOODS	SUITABLE FOODS
Fried foods, fast foods (e.g., fries, chips, fried chicken)	Sweets (without added oil)
Sugar-oil combo: cakes, doughnuts, some cookies	Fish
Dairy products: cheese, ice cream, milk, butter (particularly for lactose intolerant individuals)	Poultry (without skin)
Raw fruits and vegetables	Sparingly: olive, canola oil
Alcohol, red meats (beef/hamburger, steak, pork, lamb)	Cooking oil spray
Chocolate, soda (with caffeine), artificial fats, artificial sweeteners	Sauces without oil
Popcorn	Spices, most seasoning
Vegetable oil	Fruit/vegetables (cooked)
	Grains (cooked)
	Soy-based products

Remember: IBS often runs in cycles, so listen to your body. Whenever you feel you're catching a cold, you treat yourself to bed-rest and chicken soup. Your symptoms are treated before they get too uncomfortable for you. If you're exhausted, you might take an afternoon nap because your body and mind feel particularly sluggish. If you're able to treat your cold and take a nap, there's no reason you can't treat your GI tract by not consuming the right foods and remaining calm. These two factors alone will enable you to significantly reduce your symptoms and improve your life.

Visit your physician so you can rule out a more serious condition. Chronicle your food intake and stress inducing events. Make necessary and reasonable changes and monitor your improvements. You can live with IBS as long as you remain patient, are open to experimentation, and stay sensitive to the sounds and signs of your body. There's no need to live in shame, or embarrassment, frustration, or pain. Take your time and be sensible. Good luck, have fun, and enjoy feeling great!

▪ information ▪
and resources

The American Gastrointestinal Association
7910 Woodmont Avenue
Bethesda, MD 20814

Food and Drug Administration
500 Fishers Lane
Rockville, MD 20857

The American Heart Association
National Center
7272 Greenville Avenue
Dallas, TX 75231

The American Academy of Nutrition
3408 Sausalito
Corona Del Mar, CA 92625

The American College of Nutrition
300 South Duncan Avenue
Suite 225
Clearwater, FL 33755

The National Institute of Diabetes and Digestive and Kidney Diseases
2 Information Way
Bethesda, MD 20892

The National Academy of Sciences
Food and Nutrition Board
2101 Constitution Avenue N.W.
Washington, D.C. 20418

UNC Center for Functional Gastrointestinal and Motility Disorders
Chapel Hill, NC 27599

American Academy of Family Physicians
11400 Tomahawk Creek Parkway
Leawood, KS 66211

American Yoga Association
P.O. Box 19986
Sarasota, FL 34276

Mayo Clinic
St. Luke's Hospital
4201 Buford Road
Jacksonville, FL 32216

The Iyengar Yoga Association
27 West 24th St
Suite 800
New York, NY 10010

• diet and nutrition •
a reference guide to the foods you eat[25]

FOOD	AMOUNT	CALORIES	FAT (gm)	FIBER (gm)	PROTEIN (gm)
A					
Almonds, dried	1 oz	168	14.9	.8	5.7
Apple, with skin	1 medium	82	.5	1.1	.3
Apple butter	1 tbsp.	33	.1	.1	>1
Apple juice	1 c.	118	.3	.5	.2
Applesauce	½ c.	97	.2	.6	.2
Apricots, dried	¼ c.	77	.2	1.0	1.2
Apricots, fresh	3	51	.4	.6	1.5
Artichokes, cooked	½ c.	42	.1	1.1	2.9
Artichokes, raw	1 large	76	.3	1.9	5.3
Asparagus, fresh spears	1 c.	14	.2	.5	1.5
Avocado, California	1	305	29.9	3.6	3.6
Avocado, Florida	1	339	81.5	6.4	4.8
B					
Bacon, Canadian	2 slices	25	.8	>1	5
Bacon	3 slices	109	9.3	0	5.8
Bagel, egg	1	230	2.5	2.0	9.0
Bagel, plain	1	210	1.5	1.0	10.0
Bananas, fresh	1 medium	105	.5	.6	1.1
Barbecue sauce	2 tbsp.	60	>1	0	0
Barley, cooked	½ c.	95	.3	.2	1.8
Bass, striped, cooked	3 oz.	122	3.9	0	20.2
Beans					
baked, in tomato sauce	½ c.	123	1.3	1.5	6.5
baked, plain/vegetarian	½ c.	116	.6	1.4	6.0
Kidney, canned	1 c.	203	.8	2.5	13.0
Lima, cooked	1 c.	191	.5	0	12.2
Mung, uncooked	1 c.	31	.2	.8	3.1

[25] This chart has been compiled from a number of sources understood to be reliable. Clearly, variations in food preparation and ingredients would alter the numerical values. As a result, this chart cannot provide exact nutritional value.

FOOD	AMOUNT	CALORIES	FAT (gm)	FIBER (gm)	PROTEIN (gm)
Pinto, cooked	I c.	228	.8	5.0	13.6
Snap, yellow/green	I c.	44	.4	1.8	2.4
Other beans: black and brown	I c.	220	.8	3.4	14.8
White, cooked	I c.	232	.7	4.2	16.2
Beef					
corned, cooked	3.5 oz	209	15.8	0	15.2
Corned-beef hash	I c.	440	30	2	19
Flank steak, braised	3 oz.	203	11.5	0	23.3
Ground, extra lean	3 oz.	213	13.5	0	23.8
Ground beef, lean	3 oz.	227	15.4	0	20.6
Ground beef, regular	3 oz.	241	17.2	0	20.0
Liver, cooked	3 oz.	134	4.1	0	20.3
London broil	3 oz	162	5.4	0	26.4
Pot Roast	3 oz.	195	8.6	0	27.5
Ribs	3 oz.	194	11.3	0	21.7
Round	3 oz.	162	6.7	0	23.8
Stew, homemade with vegetables	I c.	218	10.5	>1	15.7
Stick, smoked	I	109	9.8	0	4.3
Beer	12 oz.	146	0	0	1.1
Beer, light	12 oz.	100	0	0	.7
Beets, boiled	I c.	73	.3	1.3	2.8
Beets, canned	I c.	73	.3	1.5	2.0
Beverages					
Gin, rum, whiskey, vodka	I fl.oz.	73	0	0	0
Wines, table, all	4 oz.	82	0	0	0
Club soda	12 oz.	0	0	0	0
Colas	12 oz.	152	0	0	0
Cream sodas	12 oz.	189	0	0	0
Diet colas, aspartame sweetened	12 oz.	4	0	0	.4
Fruit flavored colas	12 oz.	148	0	0	0
Fruit punch	12 oz.	195	0	0	0
Ginger ale	12 oz.	126	0	0	0
Lemonade, frozen	12 oz.	114	.1	0	>1
Lemonade, powdered	2 tbsp.	150	0	0	4.5
Root beer	12 oz.	152	0	0	0
Seltzer/carbonated water	12 oz.	0	0	0	0
Tonic water	12 oz.	125	0	0	0
Biscuits	2	190	6.5	1.8	2.0
Biscuits, with sausage and egg	I	587	39.1	.2	19.5
Blackberries/Boysenberries	I c.	75	.6	5.9	1.04
Black-eyed peas	I c.	162	.7	3.2	5.3
Blueberries	I c.	81	.6	1.9	1.0
Bluefish, cooked	3 oz.	103	3.5	0	16.7
Brazil nuts	I oz.	187	18.9	.7	4.1

FOOD	AMOUNT	CALORIES	FAT (gm)	FIBER (gm)	PROTEIN (gm)
Bread					
French, one loaf	1 slice	70	1	1.0	3.0
Italian	1 slice	70	1	1.0	3.0
Oatbran	1 slice	60	1.0	1.0	2.0
Potato	1 slice	80	1.0	1.0	3.0
Pumpernickel	1 slice	80	1.0	2.0	3.0
Raisin	1 slice	80	1.0	1.0	2.0
Rye	1 slice	80	.5	2.0	3.0
Stoneground, wholegrain	1 slice	90	1	2.0	4.0
White, enriched	1 slice	70	1.0	1.0	2.0
Whole wheat	1 slice	90	1.5	2.0	4.0
Bread crumbs, plain	1/4 c.	120	1.5	2.0	4.0
Bread pudding	1/2 c.	210	7.4	.4	6.5
Bread sticks	1/2 c.	200	9.8	1.2	3.0
Broccoli, frozen, cooked	1 c.	56	.2	2.4	6.2
Broccoli, raw	1 stalk	42	.6	1.7	4.5
Broccoli, fresh, cooked	1 stalk	47	7	1.8	5.0
Brussels sprouts, boiled	1 c.	65	.8	2.3	4.3
Bulgar wheat, cooked	1/2 c.	75	.2	.3	2.8
Butter					
salted, light	1 tbsp.	50	6.0	0	>1
Regular, salted	1 tbsp.	100	11.0	0	0
Whipped, regular	1 tbsp.	60	7.0	0	0
Buttermilk, low-fat	1 c.	100	2.3	0	8.3
C					
Cabbage, cooked	1 c.	33	.6	.9	1.5
Cabbage, raw	1 c.	18	.2	.9	1.0
Cake, packaged mix,					
Angel food	1 slice	140	0	>1	3.0
Chocolate with chocolate icing	1 slice	310	14.0	2.0	3.0
Devil's food	1 slice	250	12.0	1.0	3.0
Gingerbread	1 slice	230	7.1	>1	2.0
Marble	1 slice	250	11.0	.1	3.0
Marble, fat free	1 slice	130	0	1.0	2.0
Spice	1 slice	250	11.0	0	3.0
White	1 slice	240	10.0	0	3.0
Yellow	1 slice	250	10.0	0	1.0
Homemade, plain	1 slice	313	120	>1	3.9
Frozen, chocolate with					
chocolate icing	1 slice	250	13.0	2.0	3.0
Cake Icing, dry mix					
Chocolate	1/12 package	159	5.5	0	.5
Homemade	1/12 package	200	5.6	.2	.7
Prepared:					
Chocolate	1/12 package	153	6.8	.2	.4

FOOD	AMOUNT	CALORIES	FAT (gm)	FIBER (gm)	PROTEIN (gm)
Coconut	1/12 package	159	9.2	1.0	.6
Cream Cheese	1/12 package	159	6.7	.2	>1
Vanilla	1/12 package	161	6.5	.1	>1
Candy					
Butterscotch	1 piece	24	.2 0	>1	
Caramels	1 piece	31	.6 0	.4	
Chewing gum	1 stick	10	>1	0	0
Chocolate, squares, unsweetened	1 square	149	15.8	.7	2.9
Bittersweet	1 oz.	136	9.8	.7	2.0
Semisweet	1 oz.	136	9.1	.7	2.0
Sweet	1 oz.	132	7.7	2.0	2.2
Gumdrops	10 small	129	0	0	0
Jellybeans	10 small	40	.1	0	0
Licorice, lollipops, hard candy	1 piece	23	0	>1	0
Peanut Brittle	1 oz.	129	5.5	.4	2.1
Chocolate Bars					
coconut	1 small bar	72	4.3	0	.7
caramel, fudge, peanuts	1 small bar	68	3.3	.1	1.4
fudge	1 piece	65	1.4	>1	.3
milk chocolate, plain	1 bar	223	13.3	.2	3.0
milk chocolate with crisped rice	1 bar	198	10.6	.2	2.5
milk, with nuts	1 bar	229	15.0	.7	3.9
peanut butter cup	3 large	202	12.9	.4	4.6
Carrots fresh, cooked	1 c.	70	.3	2.3	1.7
Carrots frozen, cooked	1 c.	51	.1	1.7	1.7
Carrots raw	1 medium	31	.1	.7	.7
Cashews, dry roasted	1 oz.	164	13.3	.2	4.4
Cashews Roasted in oil	1 oz.	165	13.8	.4	4.6
Cauliflower, fresh, cooked	1 c.	29	.6	1.0	2.3
Caviar, black lumpfish	1 tbsp.	15	1.0	0	1.0
Celery, fresh, cooked	1 c.	27	.3	1.3	1.2
Celery, raw	1 stalk	6	>1	.3	.3
Chard, Swiss, cooked	1 c.	35	.2	1.6	3.3
Chard, Swiss, raw	1 c.	7	.1	.3	.6
Cheese					
American, pasteurized	1 oz.	104	8.7	0	6.2
Cheese spread, American	1 oz.	81	5.9	0	4.6
Blue/Roquefort	1 oz.	98	8.1	0	5.9
Camembert	1 oz.	83	6.7	0	5.5
Cheddar	1 oz.	112	9.2	0	6.9
Cheddar, fat-free	1 oz.	30	0	0	5
Cheddar, reduced fat	1 oz.	70	4.5	0	8
Cottage cheese	1/2 c.	116	5.1	0	14.1
Cottage cheese, low fat	1/2 c.	81	1.2	0	14.0
Cream cheese, fat free	1 oz.	29	0	0	4.0

FOOD	AMOUNT	CALORIES	FAT (gm)	FIBER (gm)	PROTEIN (gm)
Cream cheese, light	I oz.	72	6.5	0	2.8
Cream cheese	I oz.	97	9.7	0	2.1
Feta	I oz.	73	5.9	0	3.9
Mozzarella, part skim	I oz.	71	4.4	0	6.7
Mozzarella, whole milk	I oz.	78	6.0	0	5.4
Parmesan, grated	I tbsp.	23	1.5	0	2.1
Pimiento	I oz.	104	8.7	>1	6.1
Provolone	I oz.	98	7.4	0	7.1
Ricotta, part skim	¼ c.	171	9.8	0	14.1
Ricotta, whole milk	½ c.	216	16.1	0	14.0
Swiss	I oz.	93	6.9	0	6.9
Cheese puffs	I oz.	158	9.8	.1	2.2
Cherries					
maraschino	I oz.	33	1.0	.1	.1
sour, canned, water-packed	I c.	88	.2	.2	1.9
sweet, canned, water-packed	I c.	115	.3	.5	2.0
fresh, red	I c.	50	.3	.2	1.0
fresh	I c.	103	1.4	.6	1.7
Chestnuts, raw	I oz.	64	.3	.5	1.2
Chicken					
Skinless, roasted breast	½ breast	138	3.0	0	25.8
With skin, roasted	½ breast	197	7.7	0	29.2
Drumstick, skinless	I	75	2.5	0	12.3
Drumstick, with skin	I	114	5.9	0	14.2
Thigh, skinless	I	110	5.7	0	13.7
Thigh, with skin	I	154	9.7	0	15.6
Wing, skinless	I	43	1.7	0	6.4
Wing, with skin	I	100	6.7	0	9.3
Broth, canned	3 oz.	138	6.7	0	18.2
Fried	3 oz.	250	16.0	0	14.0
Chicken liver, cooked	¼ c.	54	1.9	0	8.4
Nuggets	6 pieces	220	14.0	0	13.0
Patties	I patty	190	12.0	1.0	10.0
Chicken pot pie	I pie	550	34.0	5.0	19.0
Chickpeas, cooked	½ c.	137	2.2	2.1	7.4
Chicory, raw greens	I c.	38	.5	1.3	2.8
Chili, canned, with beans	I c.	220	7.0	6.0	19.0
Chocolate, hot cocoa powdered	2-3 tsp.	76	.7	.2	.7
Chocolate milk	8 oz.	208	8.5	.2	8.0
Chocolate syrup	I tbsp.	41	.2	>1	.4
Clams, cooked	3	123	1.7	0	21.3
Clams, raw	I 2x2"	161	15.2	2.0	1.5
Cod, cooked	3 oz.	68	.6	0	14.8
Coffee, regular or decaf.	I c.	5	0	0	.3

FOOD	AMOUNT	CALORIES	FAT (gm)	FIBER (gm)	PROTEIN (gm)
Cold Cuts					
Bologna, light	1 slice	50	4.0	0	3.0
Chicken roll	1 slice	45	2.1	0	5.6
Ham, canned	1 slice	68	5.4	0	4.6
Ham, regular	1 slice	52	3.0	0	5.0
Liverwurst	1 slice	58	5.1	0	4.6
Olive loaf	1 slice	67	4.7	0	3.4
Pastrami	1 slice	43	2.3	0	5.3
Salami	1 slice	59	4.7	0	3.4
Turkey or chicken breast	1 slice	23	.3	0	4.7
Turkey bologna	1 slice	57	4.3	0	3.9
Turkey ham	1 slice	37	1.5	0	5.4
Turkey pastrami	1 slice	40	1.8	0	5.3
Turkey salami	1 slice	56	3.9	0	4.7
Coleslaw	½ c.	41	1.5	.4	.8
Collard, greens, cooked	1 c.	34	.3	.6	1.8
Cookies, packaged mix					
Chocolate chip	1	160	7.2	.5	2.0
Brownies	1	200	9.0	1.0	1.0
Cookies, boxed					
Animal crackers	14	140	4.0	>1	2.0
Chocolate chip	3	160	8.0	1.0	2.0
Chocolate chip, reduced fat	3	150	6.0	>1	2.0
Coconut bars	4	140	5.0	1.0	2.0
Fig bars	2	110	2.5	1.0	1.0
Gingersnaps	4	120	2.5	>1	1.0
Graham crackers,					
Chocolate covered	3	140	7.0	>1	1.0
Plain	2 whole	120	3.5	>1	1.0
Oatmeal	1 large	80	3	>1	1.0
Oatmeal raisin	2	110	5	1.0	1.0
Sandwich cookie, creme filled					
Chocolate or vanilla	3	150	7.0	1.0	2.0
Chocolate, crème filled,					
Reduced fat	3	140	5.0	1.0	2.0
Devil's food, cookie cakes, fat-free	1	50	0	>1	1.0
Peanut butter	2	130	6.0	1.0	3.0
Shortbread	4	140	7.0	>1	2.0
Sugar wafers, with filling	5	140	7.0	>1	>1
Vanilla wafers	8	140	5.0	0	2.0
Corn					
Creamed, canned	1 c.	180	1.0	1.3	4.3
Whole kernel, canned	1 c.	135	1.7	0	4.3
Fresh, on the cob or kernels	1 medium	83	1	.5	2.5
Frozen, on the cob, cooked	1 medium	58	.4	.4	1.9

FOOD	AMOUNT	CALORIES	FAT (gm)	FIBER (gm)	PROTEIN (gm)
Frozen, on the cob, cooked	1 c.	135	.2	.8	5.0
Corn bread, homemade	1 piece	161	5.6	>1	5.8
Corn bread, packages	1 piece	180	5.6	1.3	2.0
Corn chips	1 oz.	154	9.5	.3	1.9
Corn grits, cooked	1 c.	150	.5	.3	3.5
Corn flakes, cereal	1 c.	110	0	1.0	2.0
Corn flakes, cereal with sugar	1 c.	156	0	0	1.3
Cornstarch	1 tbsp.	29	>1	0	>1
Cow peas or Black-eyed peas	1 c.	162	.7	3.2	5.3
Crab, Alaskan king, cooked	3 oz.	81	1.3	0	16.2
Crab, cakes	3.5 oz.	93	4.5	>1	12.1
Crabapple	1 c.	84	.3	.7	.4
Crackers					
Cheese	27 small	160	8.0	>1	4.0
Rye wafers	2	60	0	4.0	2.0
Saltines	5	60	1.5	>1	2.0
Sandwich, cheese with					
peanut butter filling	6	200	11.0	1.0	4.0
Thin wheat	16	140	6.0	2.0	3.0
Thin wheat, low sodium	16	140	4.0	1.0	2.0
Water cracker	5	45	0	1.0	2.0
Whole wheat	7	140	5.0	4.0	3.0
Cranberries	1 c.	47	.2	1.1	.4
Cranberry juice cocktail	1 c.	145	.1	0	.1
Cranberry sauce, canned	1 c.	378	.4	.8	.5
Cream					
Half and half	1 tbsp.	20	1.7	0	.4
Heavy, unwhipped	1 tbsp.	51	5.5	0	.3
Heavy, whipped, canned	1 tbsp.	20	1.5	0	0
Light, table	1 tbsp.	29	2.9	0	.4
Cream, substitute, powered	1 tsp.	11	.7	0	.1
Cucumber	1 medium	40	.3	1.8	2.1
Currants, black	3.5 oz.	32	.2	1.2	.7
Currants, red or white	3.5 oz.	28	.1	1.7	.7
Custard, egg, homemade	½ c.	150	6.7	0	7.3
D					
Dandelion greens, raw	1 c.	25	.4	.9	1.5
Dates	5	115	.2	.9	.8
Doughnuts, low fat	1	220	6.0	>1	2.0
Doughnuts, regular, plain	1	170	9.0	>1	3.0
Duck, cooked, skinless	¼ duck	223	12.4	0	26.1
Duck, cooked, with skin	¼ duck	674	56.8	0	38.0

FOOD	AMOUNT	CALORIES	FAT (gm)	FIBER (gm)	PROTEIN (gm)
E					
Eel, cooked	3 oz.	197	12.5	0	19.8
Eggnog	1 c.	343	19	0	9.7
Eggplant, cooked	1 c.	28	.2	1.0	.8
Eggs					
Fried, in butter	1	83	6.4	0	5.4
Hard, soft boiled, raw or poached	1	79	5.6	0	6.1
Scrambled	1	93	5.8	0	5.8
Whites only, raw	1	16	>1	0	3.4
Yolks only, raw	1	63	5.6	0	2.8
Substitute	2 oz., 1 egg	53	2.1	0	7.6
Endive or escarole	1 c.	9	.1	.5	.6
F					
Farina, cooked	1 c.	117	.2	0	3.3
Figs, canned in syrup	½ c.	86	.1	.8	.6
Figs, fresh	1	37	.2	.6	.4
Filberts, hazelnuts, dried	1 oz.	181	17.9	1.1	3.7
Fish sticks, frozen, breaded	5 sticks	389	17.4	.6	22.4
Fish sticks, reduced fat	6 sticks	180	3.0	0	13
Flatfish, cooked	3 oz.	98	1.3	0	20.2
Flounder, cooked	3 oz.	98	1.3	1.3	20.2
Frankfurters, beef	1 frank	175	15.8	0	6.7
Frankfurters, beef, low fat	1 frank	60	1.5	0	7.0
Frankfurters, chicken/turkey	1 frank	142	10.8	0	7.2
French toast, with butter	2 slices	377	20.0	.1	11.0
Frozen fruit bars	1	63	.1	0	.9
Frozen pudding pops	1	73	2.2	>1	1.9
Fruit cocktail, canned in heavy syrup	½ c.	91	.1	.6	.5
G					
Garlic, raw	1 clove	5	>1	>1	.2
Gelatin desserts, reduced calorie, aspartame sweetened	1 c.	16	0	0	0
Gelatin desserts, regular	1 c.	159	0	0	3.2
Goose, skinless, cooked	1/16 goose	170	9.1	0	20.7
Goose, with skin, cooked	1/16 goose	305	21.9	0	25.1
Granola, with almonds and seeds	⅓ c.	220	9.0	4.0	6.0
Granola bars, hard	1 oz. bar	135	5.7	.3	2.9
Granola bars, soft, low fat	1 oz. bar	110	2.0	1.0	2.0
Grapefruit, canned, light syrup	½ c.	75	.1	.4	.8
Grapefruit, fresh, white, pink or red	½	40	.1	.3	.8
Grapefruit juice, sweetened	1 c.	115	.3	0	1.5
Grapefruit juice, unsweetened	1 c.	95	.3	0	1.3

FOOD	AMOUNT	CALORIES	FAT (gm)	FIBER (gm)	PROTEIN (gm)
Grapefruit juice, fresh	I c.	98	.3	0	1.3
Grapefruit juice, frozen	I c.	103	.3	0	1.4
Grape juice, canned	I c.	153	.2	.8	1.5
Grape juice, frozen	I c.	128	.2	.3	.5
Grapes, American	I c.	58	.3	.7	.6
Gravy, canned, turkey	¼ c.	30	1.2	>1	1.5
Gravy, dry mix	¼ c.	20	0	0	1.0
Guavas	I	46	.5	5.1	.7
Guinea hen, with skin	¼ hen	362	18.6	0	45.4

H

Haddock, cooked	3 oz.	93	.8	0	20.2
Halibut, cooked	3 oz.	116	2.4	0	22.3
Herring, pickled	3 pieces	119	8.2	0	6.5
Hickory nuts, dried	I oz.	188	18.4	.9	3.6
Honey	I tbsp.	63	0	0	.1
Horseradish	I tbsp.	0	0	0	0

I

Ice cream and custard, regular	½ c.	135	7.2	0	2.4
Ice cream, rich	½ c.	174	11.9	0	2.1
Ice cream, soft-serve, vanilla	½ c.	188	11.2	0	3.5
Ice milk, hard	½ c.	92	12.6	0	2.6
Ice milk, soft-serve	½ c.	112	2.3	0	4.0
Ice milk, fat free	½ c.	90	0	0	4.0
Ices	½ c.	70	0	0	4.0

J

Jams and preserves	I tbsp.	48	>1	.1	.1
Jellies	I tbsp.	51	>1	.1	.1
Jerusalem artichoke, raw	I c.	113	>1	1.2	3.0

K

Kale, cooked	I c.	42	.5	1.0	2.5
Ketchup	I packet	6	>1	.1	.1
Kiwi	I	47	.3	.8	.8
Kumquats, fresh	3 small	36	.1	2.1	.5

L

Lake herring, smoked	3 oz.	148	9.9	0	13.7
Lamb					
cubes, lean, cooked	3 oz.	155	6.1	0	23.4
ground, cooked	3 oz.	236	16.4	0	20.7
leg, lean, cooked	3 oz.	159	6.4	0	23.6
loin, lean, cooked	3 oz.	168	8.2	0	22.2

FOOD	AMOUNT	CALORIES	FAT (gm)	FIBER (gm)	PROTEIN (gm)
shoulder, lean, cooked	3 oz.	170	9.0	0	20.8
Lard	I tbsp.	116	12.8	0	0
Leeks, raw	2	153	.8	3.8	3.8
Lemon juice, bottled	I c.	53	.8	0	1.0
Lemon juice, fresh	I c.	63	0	0	1.0
Lemons, fresh	I medium	17	.2	.2	.6
Lentils, cooked	I c.	232	.8	5.6	18.4
Lettuce, butter	I head	22	.4	0	2.2
Lettuce, iceberg	I head	68	1.1	2.6	5.2
Lettuce, romaine	2 leaves	4	.1	.1	.3
Lime juice, fresh or concentrate	I c.	68	.3	0	1.0
Limeade, concentrate	I c.	103	0	0	0
Limes, fresh	I medium	20	.1	.3	.5
Lobster, cooked	3 oz.	82	.5	0	17.1
Loganberries, frozen	I c.	79	.4	0	2.1
M					
Macadamia nuts, dried	I oz.	200	21.1	1.5	2.4
Mackerel, Atlantic, cooked	3 oz.	218	14.8	0	19.9
Mangoes, fresh	I small	135	.6	1.7	1.0
Margarine, nonfat, soft	I tbsp.	20	2.0	0	0
Margarine, stick, regular	I tbsp.	101	11.3	0	.1
Margarine, soybean, reduced fat	I tbsp.	50	6.0	0	.1
Marmalade	I tbsp.	49	0	0	.1
Mayonnaise, low fat	I tbsp.	25	1.0	0	0
Mayonnaise, regular	I tbsp.	99	11.0	0	.2
Melons, fresh					
Cantaloupe	½ melon	88	.8	1.0	2.2
Casaba	¹⁄₁₀ melon	43	.2	.8	1.5
Honeydew	¹⁄₁₀ melon	44	.1	.8	.6
Milk					
Canned, condensed, sweetened	½ c.	491	13.4	0	12.1
Dry, skim, instant	I c.	244	.5	0	24.9
Dry, skim, regular	I c.	434	.9	0	43.4
Dry, whole	I c.	635	34.2	0	33.7
Evaporated, unsweetened	½ c.	169	9.6	0	8.6
Evaporated, skimmed	½ c.	100	.3	0	9.7
Malted, powder	3 tsp.	86	1.6	0	2.3
Cow's, low fat, 2 %	I c.	122	4.6	0	8.1
Cow's, skim	I c.	86	.4	0	8.4
Cow's, whole	I c.	484	8.1	0	8.1
Goat's	I c.	168	10.1	0	8.7
Human's	I c.	172	10.8	0	2.5
Molasses	I tbsp.	53	>1	0	0
Muffins, flour, fat free	I	120	0	>1	2.0

FOOD	AMOUNT	CALORIES	FAT (gm)	FIBER (gm)	PROTEIN (gm)
Muffins, homemade, blueberry	1	112	3.7	>1	2.9
Muffins, packaged mix	1	140	5.0	0	2.0
Mushrooms, canned	½ c.	19	.2	0	1.5
Mushrooms, fresh	½ c.	9	.1	.3	.7
Mussels, cooked	3 oz.	143	3.8	0	19.8
Mustard, prepared	1 tsp.	0	0	0	0
Mustard greens, cooked	1 c.	21	.3	1.0	3.3
N					
Nectarines, fresh	1 medium	66	.7	.6	1.2
Nuts, see individual names					
O					
Oatmeal, instant, maple flavored	1 c.	380	4.0	6.0	12.0
Oatmeal, rolled oats, cooked	1 c.	144	2.3	.5	6.0
Oats, flaked	1 c.	156	2.0	1.3	2.6
Oils					
Canola	1 tbsp.	130	13.5	0	0
Corn	1 tbsp.	119	13.5	0	0
Olive	1 tbsp.	119	13.5	0	0
Safflower/sunflower	1 tbsp.	119	13.5	0	0
Okra, cooked	10 pods	36	.2	1.0	2.1
Olives, canned, small	3	15	1.4	0	.1
Olives, jumbo	3	37	3.1	0	.5
Onion powder	1 tsp.	7	>1	.1	.2
Onions, boiled	½ c.	46	.2	.7	1.5
Onions, raw	½ c.	30	.1	.5	1.0
Orange drink, powered	1 tbsp.	92	>1	0	>1
Orange juice, canned	1 c.	105	.3	.3	1.5
Orange juice, fresh	1 c.	113	.5	.3	1.8
Orange juice, frozen, concentrate	1 c.	113	.2	.1	1.8
Oranges, fresh, peeled	1 medium	62	.1	.5	1.2
Oranges, Navels	1 medium	66	.1	.7	1.4
Oranges, Valencias	1 medium	59	.4	.6	1.2
Oysters, cooked	6	57	2.0	0	5.9
P					
Pancakes, packaged mix	2 cakes	170	6.0	>1	3.0
Pancakes, packaged mix, reduced fat	2 cakes	150	2.5	>1	3.0
Papaya, fresh	1	130	.5	2.7	2.0
Parsley, raw	1 tbsp.	4	.1	.1	.3
Parsnips, cooked	1 c.	135	.5	3.7	2.2
Pasta					
Cooked	1 c.	201	1.0	.1	6.9
Egg	1 c.	222	2.5	.2	8.0

FOOD	AMOUNT	CALORIES	FAT (gm)	FIBER (gm)	PROTEIN (gm)
Spinach	1 c.	186	.9	1.7	6.6
Pastina	2 oz.	210	2.5	2.0	10.0
Peaches, canned, heavy syrup	½ c.	93	.1	.4	.6
Peaches, canned, light syrup	½ c.	68	>1	.4	.6
Peaches, fresh	1 medium	37	.1	.5	.6
Peanut butter	1 tbsp.	93	7.9	.4	3.9
Peanuts, fresh, unsalted	1 oz.	163	13.8	1.4	6.6
Pears, canned in heavy syrup	½ c.	93	.2	.8	.3
Pears, canned in light syrup	½ c.	71	>1	.8	.3
Pears, fresh	1 medium	98	.7	2.3	.7
Peas, canned, cooked	1 c.	115	.6	3.3	7.3
Peas, fresh, cooked	1 c.	140	.4	3.8	9.0
Peas, frozen, cooked	1 c.	130	.5	3.5	8.6
Pecans, dried	1 oz.	191	19.3	.5	2.2
Pepperoni	1 slice	27	2.4	0	1.2
Peppers, chili, canned, cooked	½ c.	17	.1	.8	.6
Peppers, hot chili, raw	1 pepper	18	.1	.8	.9
Peppers, sweet, raw	½ c.	14	.1	.2	.4
Perch, cooked	3 oz.	98	1.0	0	20.8
Persimmons	1 small	117	.3	2.5	1.0
Pheasant	¼ pheasant	222	6.0	0	39.3
Pickle relish, sweet	1 tbsp.	19	.1	.1	.1
Pickles, dill	1 large	12	.1	.4	.4
Pickles, sour	1 medium	4	.1	.2	.1
Pickles, sweet	1 large	40	.1	.2	.1
Pies, 1 piece = ⅐ of a 9" pie					
Apple	1 piece	300	14.0	2.0	2.0
Boston cream	1 piece	170	5.0	0	2.0
Chocolate cream	1 piece	290	14.0	1.0	2.0
Coconut custard	1 piece	280	12.0	0	7.9
Lemon meringue	1 piece	270	6.0	1.0	3.0
Mince	1 piece	320	13.6	>1	3.0
Pecan	1 piece	431	23.6	>1	5.3
Pig's feet, pickled	3 oz.	169	13.4	0	11.3
Pike, cooked	3 oz.	94	.8	0	20.6
Pimientos, canned	1 tbsp.	3	>1	.1	.1
Pineapple, canned in heavy syrup	2 slices	91	.1	.5	.4
Pineapple, canned in light syrup	2 slices	60	.1	.5	.4
Pineapple, fresh	1 c.	75	.6	.8	.6
Pineapple juice, canned	1 c.	140	.2	.3	.8
Pistachio nuts, dry roasted	1 oz.	173	15.1	.5	4.3
Pita bread, large	1	150	1.0	1.0	6.0
Pita bread, small	1	70	0	>1	3.0
Pizza, with cheese	1 slice	139	3.2	.3	7.6
Pizza, with meat and vegetables	1 slice	185	5.4	.8	13.1

FOOD	AMOUNT	CALORIES	FAT (gm)	FIBER (gm)	PROTEIN (gm)
Plums, canned in heavy syrup	½ c.	111	.1	.4	.5
Plums, fresh	1 medium	37	.4	.4	.5
Pollack, cooked	3 oz.	98	1.1	0	20.8
Pomegranates, fresh	1 medium	105	.5	.3	1.5
Popcorn					
air-popped	1 c.	31	.3	.3	1.0
caramel	1 c.	154	4.6	.6	1.4
low fat, microwave	1 c.	23	1.0	0	.7
regular, microwave	1 c.	33	2.0	0	.7
oil-popped	1 c.	55	3.1	.4	1.0
Pork					
Boston blade, fresh					
Roasted, lean	3 oz.	213	14.0	0	20.3
Ham, canned, lean	3 oz.	113	4.1	0	17.7
Ham, cured, fresh	3 oz.	131	4.6	0	20.9
Ham steak, fresh, boneless	3 oz.	102	3.6	0	16.3
Loin, fresh, lean	3 oz.	200	11.5	0	22.4
Sirloin, fresh, lean	3 oz.	196	11.0	0	22.9
Spareribs, fresh, lean	3 oz.	331	25.3	0	24.3
Potato Chips					
Barbecue	1 oz.	140	9.3	.5	2.2
Plain	1 oz.	153	9.9	.5	2.0
Reduced fat	1 oz.	150	10.0	1.0	2.0
Low sodium	1 oz.	130	6.0	1.0	2.0
Potatoes					
Baked or microwaved, with skin	1 medium	218	.2	1.3	4.6
Boiled, with skin	1 medium	119	.1	.4	2.6
Canned, drained	1 c.	109	.4	.5	2.5
Chips, homemade	1 oz.	153	9.9	.5	2.0
French-fried in vegetable oil	10 pieces	158	8.3	.4	2.0
Pretzels, hard, plain	1 oz.	109	1.0	.1	2.6
Prunes					
juice	1 c.	178	.1	>1	1.5
dried	1 c.	213	.4	1.9	2.6
dried, softened	1 c.	398	.8	3.3	4.3
Puddings, instant, dry mix	½ c.	146	2.7	.1	4.4
Puddings, dry mix, sugar free	½ c.	70	0	0	0
Puddings, dry mix, regular	½ c.	151	2.9	.3	4.7
Pumpkin, canned	1 c.	85	.8	4.0	2.8
Pumpkin and squash seeds, roasted	1 oz.	127	5.5	10.3	5.3
Q					
Quail, with skin	½ quail	107	6.7	0	10.9

FOOD	AMOUNT	CALORIES	FAT (gm)	FIBER (gm)	PROTEIN (gm)

R

FOOD	AMOUNT	CALORIES	FAT (gm)	FIBER (gm)	PROTEIN (gm)
Rabbit, cooked	3 oz.	144	2.9	0	27.5
Radishes, raw	4	3	.1	.1	.1
Raisins, raw	1 c.	503	.8	2.3	5.7
Raspberries, fresh	1 c.	61	.7	3.8	1.1
Raspberries, frozen	1 c.	258	.4	5.5	1.8
Rhubarb, frozen, cooked,					
Rhubarb, added sugar	½ c	140	.1	1.0	.5
Rhubarb, uncooked	1 c.	26	.2	.9	1.1
Rice					
Brown, cooked	1 c.	222	1.8	.7	5.2
Instant, cooked	1 c.	163	.3	.2	3.5
White, enriched, cooked	1 c.	217	.5	.2	4.5
Wild, cooked	1 c.	168	.5	.5	6.7
Pudding	½ c.	160	2.3	0	4.7
Rolls					
Homemade	1	119	3.0	>1	2.9
Packaged, oven baked	1	70	1.0	1.0	2.0
Crescent, refrigerated dough	1	80	3.0	1.0	2.0
Danish pastry, cheese	1	260	14.0	.1	4.0
Frankfurter/ hamburger buns	1	110	2.0	1.0	4.0
Hard rolls	1	156	1.6	>1	4.9
Raisin rolls	1	280	8.0	1.0	5.0
Rutabagas, cooked	½ c.	33	.2	1.0	1.1

S

Salad Dressings

FOOD	AMOUNT	CALORIES	FAT (gm)	FIBER (gm)	PROTEIN (gm)
Low fat					
Blue cheese	1 tbsp.	400	4.0	0	5
French/Russian	1 tbsp.	22	1.0	>1	>1
Italian	1 tbsp.	16	>1	>1	>1
Ranch/Creamy Italian	1 tbsp.	40	3.0	0	0
Nonfat					
Blue cheese	1 tbsp.	10	0	0	0
French/Russian	1 tbsp.	15	0	0	0
Italian	1 tbsp.	10	0	0	0
Ranch/Creamy Italian	1 tbsp.	20	0	0	0
Regular					
Blue cheese	1 tbsp.	78	8.0	>1	.7
French/Russian	1 tbsp.	66	6.3	.1	.1
Italian	1 tbsp.	69	7.1	>1	.1
Sandwich spread					
Low-fat	1 tbsp.	25	1.0	0	0
Nonfat	1 tbsp.	10	0	0	0
Regular	1 tbsp.	99	11.0	0	.2

FOOD	AMOUNT	CALORIES	FAT (gm)	FIBER (gm)	PROTEIN (gm)
Salmon, canned, pink	3 oz.	116	5.1	0	16.5
Salmon, fresh	3 oz.	124	3.7	0	21.3
Salt, table	1 tsp.	0	0	0	0
Sardines, canned, in tomato sauce	1	68	4.6	>1	6.3
Sauce, Bearnaise	¼ c.	172	16.8	>1	2.1
Sauce, Hollandaise	¼ c.	173	16.8	>1	2.1
Sauerkraut, canned	1 c.	48	.4	2.8	2.3
Sausage					
Bratwurst, cooked	1 link	251	21.6	0	11.8
Brown and serve type	3 links	260	25.0	0	7.0
Italian, cooked	1 link	215	17.1	0	13.3
Knockwurst	1 link	205	18.5	0	7.9
Polish	½ link	362	31.9	0	15.7
Pork, cooked	1 link	48	4.1	0	2.6
Turkey	1 link	140	8.0	0	18.0
Vienna, canned	1	44	4.0	0	1.6
Scallops, raw	5 small	27	.2	0	5.1
Sea bass, cooked	3 oz.	103	2.2	0	19.7
Sesame seeds, dried	1 tbsp.	47	4.4	.2	2.1
Shad, cooked	3 oz.	210	14.8	0	18.1
Shallots, raw	1 tbsp.	7	>1	.1	1.3
Sherbet, orange	½ c.	135	1.9	>1	1.1
Shrimp, cooked	4 large	90	1.0	0	19.0
Snapper, cooked	3 oz.	106	1.4	0	21.9
Soup					
Asparagus, cream of	1 c.	88	4.3	.8	2.3
Beef broth	1 c.	18	.5	>1	2.8
Beef noodle	1 c.	85	3.3	>1	5.0
Celery, cream of	1 c.	93	5.8	.5	1.8
Chicken, cream of	1 c.	120	7.5	.1	3.5
Chicken broth	1 c.	40	1.5	>1	5.0
Chicken gumbo	1 c.	58	1.5	.3	2.8
Chicken noodle	1 c.	78	2.5	.3	4.3
Chicken vegetable	1 c.	78	3.0	.1	3.8
Chicken with rice	1 c.	63	2.0	>1	3.8
Clam chowder, Manhattan	1 c.	80	2.3	.5	2.3
Lentil	1 c.	140	2.0	7.0	9.0
Minestrone	1 c.	85	2.5	.8	4.5
Mushroom, cream of	1 c.	133	9.3	.5	2.5
Onion	1 c.	60	1.8	.5	4.0
Pea, green	1 c.	165	3.0	.8	8.5
Pea, green with ham	1 c.	188	4.3	.8	10.3
Tomato	1 c.	88	2.0	.5	2.0
Vegetable	1 c.	75	2.0	.5	2.3
Sour cream	1 tbsp.	26	2.5	0	.4

FOOD	AMOUNT	CALORIES	FAT (gm)	FIBER (gm)	PROTEIN (gm)
Soybean curd (tofu), raw	½ c.	95	6.0	.1	10.1
Soybeans, cooked	1 c.	74	4.1	1.8	7.7
Soy sauce	1 tbsp.	10	1.5	0	.9
Spinach, canned	1 c.	49	1.1	0	6.0
Spinach, cooked	1 c.	41	.5	1.6	5.4
Spinach, frozen	1 c.	54	.4	2.1	6.0
Spinach, raw	1 c.	12	.2	.5	1.6
Squash, summer cooked	1 c.	36	.5	1.1	1.6
Squash, winter	1 c.	78	1.3	1.4	1.8
Strawberries, fresh	1 c.	45	.6	.7	.9
Strawberries, frozen	½ c.	120	.2	.8	.6
Sturgeon, cooked	3 oz.	113	4.3	0	17.3
Sugar					
Beet, cane, brown	1 oz.	104	0	0	0
Granulated	1 tsp.	15	0	0	0
Powdered	1 oz.	58	>1	0	0
Maple	1 oz.	101	.1	0	>1
Sweet potatoes, baked in skin	1 medium	118	.1	.9	2.0
Sweet potatoes, candied	1 piece	144	3.5	.4	.9
Swordfish, cooked	3 oz.	129	4.3	0	21.2
Syrup					
Cane, maple, blends	1 tbsp.	53	0	0	0
High fructose, corn	1 tbsp.	53	0	0	0
Maple	1 tbsp.	52	>1	0	0
Maple, reduced calorie	1 tbsp.	28	0	0	0
T					
Tangerines, raw	1 medium	37	.2	.3	.5
Tangerine juice canned	1 c.	125	.5	.3	1.3
Tapioca pudding	½ c.	149	2.4	0	4.1
Tartar sauce, low calorie	2 tbsp.	110	11.0	0	0
Tartar sauce, regular	2 tbsp.	180	19.0	0	0
Tomato juice, canned, regular	8 oz.	21	.1	.5	1.0
Tomato paste, canned	¼ c.	53	.6	.6	2.4
Tomato puree, canned	1 c.	103	.3	2.0	4.3
Tomato sauce, canned	1 c.	75	.5	1.8	3.3
Tomato, marinara, canned	1 c.	170	8.5	1.7	4.0
Tomatoes, whole, canned	1 c.	50	.5	1.3	2.3
Tomatoes, cooked	1 c.	68	1.0	2.0	2.8
Tomatoes raw	1 medium	26.2	.4	.9	1.1
Tongue, beef, cooked	3 oz.	236	17.3	0	18.4
Trout, cooked	3 oz.	158	7.1	0	22.2
Tuna					
Chunk light in oil, canned	3 oz.	165	9.0	0	20.0
Chunk light in water, canned	3 oz.	90	.8	0	20.0
White, in oil	3 oz.	135	4.5	0	22.1

FOOD	AMOUNT	CALORIES	FAT (gm)	FIBER (gm)	PROTEIN (gm)
White, in water	3 oz.	105	1.5	0	22.5
Bluefin, fresh, cooked	3 oz.	153	5.3	0	24.9
Turkey					
dark meat, skinless	3 oz.	147	3.9	0	26.2
dark meat, with skin	3 oz.	165	6.5	0	25.2
light meat, skinless	3 oz.	127	1.1	0	27.5
light meat, with skin	3 oz.	149	4.1	0	26.2
Turnip greens, cooked	1 c.	30	.2	1.2	1.2
Turnips, raw	1 c.	36	.1	1.2	1.2
V					
Veal, cubed for stew, lean	3 oz.	157	3.6	0	29.2
Veal, ground, cooked	3 oz.	143	6.3	0	20.3
Loin, lean, cooked	3 oz.	146	5.8	0	21.9
Sirloin, lean, cooked	3 oz.	140	5.2	0	21.9
Vegetable juice cocktail	8 oz.	23	.1	.2	.7
Vegetable shortening	1 tbsp.	113	12.8	0	0
Venison, cooked	3 oz.	132	2.6	0	25.2
Vinegar, cider or white	½ oz.	2	0	0	0
W					
Waffles, frozen	2	200	7.0	2.0	4.0
Walnuts, dried	1 oz.	183	17.7	1.3	4.1
Water chestnuts, raw	½ c.	66	.1	.5	.9
Watercress, raw	½ c.	2	>1	.1	.4
Watermelon	1 c.	51	.6	.5	1.0
Wheat flour, white	1 c.	455	1.3	.4	12.9
Wheat germ	⅛ c.	50	1.4	.3	3.8
Whitefish, cooked	3 oz.	143	6.3	0	20.4
Y					
Yogurt					
fruit, low fat	1 c.	255	2.8	.3	11.0
sugar free	1 c.	100	0	0	9.0
frozen, low fat	½ c.	160	2.0	6.0	4.0
soft-serve, vanilla	1 c.	227	8.0	.1	5.7
plain, low fat	1 c.	143	3.5	0	11.9
non-fat	1 c.	127	.4	0	12.9
whole milk	1 c.	138	7.4	0	7.9
Z					
Zucchini, cooked	1 c.	29	.1	.9	1.1

· index ·